Tax Co-operation: Towards a Level Playing Field

2007 ASSESSMENT BY THE GLOBAL FORUM ON TAXATION

OECD

ORGANISATION FOR ECONOMIC CO-OPERATION AND DEVELOPMENT

The OECD is a unique forum where the governments of 30 democracies work together to address the economic, social and environmental challenges of globalisation. The OECD is also at the forefront of efforts to understand and to help governments respond to new developments and concerns, such as corporate governance, the information economy and the challenges of an ageing population. The Organisation provides a setting where governments can compare policy experiences, seek answers to common problems, identify good practice and work to co-ordinate domestic and international policies.

The OECD member countries are: Australia, Austria, Belgium, Canada, the Czech Republic, Denmark, Finland, France, Germany, Greece, Hungary, Iceland, Ireland, Italy, Japan, Korea, Luxembourg, Mexico, the Netherlands, New Zealand, Norway, Poland, Portugal, the Slovak Republic, Spain, Sweden, Switzerland, Turkey, the United Kingdom and the United States. The Commission of the European Communities takes part in the work of the OECD.

OECD Publishing disseminates widely the results of the Organisation's statistics gathering and research on economic, social and environmental issues, as well as the conventions, guidelines and standards agreed by its members.

This work is published on the responsibility of the Secretary-General of the OECD. The opinions expressed and arguments employed herein do not necessarily reflect the official views of the Organisation or of the governments of its member countries.

Also available in French under the title:
Coopération fiscale 2007 : Vers l'établissement de règles du jeu équitables
ÉVALUATION PAR LE FORUM MONDIAL SUR LA FISCALITÉ

Foreword

This report has been prepared by the OECD's Global Forum on Taxation, which includes both OECD and non-OECD economies. In 2006, the Global Forum on Taxation published a review of 82 economies' legal and administrative frameworks in the areas of transparency and exchange of information for tax purposes entitled, Tax Co-operation: Towards a Level Playing Field - 2006 Assessment by the Global Forum on Taxation. This report updates the information contained in the 2006 Assessment as of 1 January 2007.

Table of contents

I. Introduction

1.	In May 2006, the OECD published a report, *Tax Co-operation: Towards a Level Playing Field - 2006 Assessment by the Global Forum on Taxation* (hereafter referred to as the 2006 Report). The report was prepared by the OECD's Global Forum on Taxation,[1] which includes both OECD and non-OECD countries,[2] in connection with its work aimed at determining what is required to achieve a global level playing field in the areas of transparency and effective exchange of information for tax purposes. In working towards the achievement of a global level playing field in these areas, the Global Forum seeks to ensure the implementation of high standards of transparency and exchange of information, for both civil and criminal taxation matters, within an acceptable timeline with the aim of achieving equity and fair competition.

2.	The 2006 Report represents a major achievement for the Global Forum on Taxation. It reflects the outcome of a factual review carried out by the Global Forum on the legal and administrative frameworks in the areas of transparency and exchange of information in over 80 countries.[3]

3.	One of the features of the 2006 Report was to describe and summarise the principles of transparency and effective exchange of information for tax purposes.[4] These are summarised in the 2006 report as follows:

Key Principles of Transparency and Information Exchange for Tax Purposes

- Existence of mechanisms for exchange of information upon request.
- Exchange of information for purposes of domestic tax law in both criminal and civil matters.
- No restrictions of information exchange caused by application of dual criminality principle or domestic tax interest requirement.
- Respect for safeguards and limitations.
- Strict confidentiality rules for information exchanged.
- Availability of reliable information (in particular bank, ownership, identity and accounting information) and powers to obtain and provide such information in response to a specific request.

---

[1] The OECD carries out its dialogue on tax issues with non-OECD economies under the multilateral framework known as the "Global Forum on Taxation". The composition of the Global Forum generally varies depending on the topics covered by the meeting. The Global Forum referred to in this report includes the countries participating in efforts to work towards a level playing field in the areas of transparency and exchange of information in tax matters (collectively referred to as Participating Partners). A different group of countries is involved in the Global Forum's work on tax treaties and transfer pricing.

[2] References in this document and its annexes and tables to "countries" should be taken to apply equally to "territories", "dependencies" or "jurisdictions". See Annex I for a list of Global Forum Participating Partners and other countries covered by this factual assessment.

[3] Three countries (Antigua and Barbuda, Brunei and Grenada) did not respond to the questionnaire used to prepare the 2006 Report. The information contained in the 2006 Report regarding these countries was obtained from publicly available sources, or information previously provided by Antigua and Barbuda and Grenada.

[4] The principles of transparency and effective information exchange for tax purposes have been articulated and refined through the work of the Global Forum. They are reflected in the Model Agreement on Exchange of Information in Tax Matters (Model Agreement), which was released in 2002, and in the work that the Global Forum has done in connection with ensuring the availability of reliable accounting information through its Joint Ad Hoc Group on Accounts. The principles reflected in the Model Agreement are also found in Article 26 of the OECD Model Tax Convention on Income and on Capital.

4.   All of the OECD and non-OECD Participating Partners in the Global Forum on Taxation have endorsed the principles of transparency and exchange of information for tax purposes that are reflected in the 2006 Report. At its Melbourne meeting, in November 2005, the Global Forum also welcomed the endorsement of these principles by Argentina; China; Hong Kong, China; Macao, China; the Russian Federation and South Africa. In April 2007, the United Arab Emirates announced its endorsement of the principles. More recently, Liberia made a commitment to the principles of transparency and effective exchange of information for tax purposes and was removed from the OECD's List of Unco-operative Tax Havens on 24 July 2007. The Global Forum's efforts to promote high standards of transparency and exchange of information are also strongly supported by international organisations, including the G-8,[5] the G-20[6] and the European Union.

5.   The 2006 Report showed that both OECD and non-OECD countries had implemented or made considerable progress towards implementing the transparency and effective exchange of information standards that the Global Forum wishes to see achieved. It also showed that further progress is needed if a global level playing field is to be achieved. Thus, the Statement of Outcomes issued after the Global Forum meeting in Melbourne on 15-16 November 2005 outlined a series of steps involving individual, bilateral and collective actions which would be needed to both achieve and maintain the goal of a level playing field.[7]

6.   In terms of individual actions, countries were encouraged to modify existing laws and practices, where necessary, to fully implement the principles of transparency and exchange of information for tax purposes. Further, they were asked to review their policies in relation to six areas in particular and report the outcome of their reviews at the next meeting of the Global Forum.[8] The Global Forum has not met since the Melbourne meeting; thus outcomes of those reviews are not reflected in this report unless they resulted in changes to countries' legal and administrative frameworks for transparency and exchange of information before 1 January 2007.

7.   In terms of bilateral actions, the Global Forum has recognised that the principle of effective exchange of information for civil and criminal tax matters will generally be implemented through a process of bilateral negotiations. Accordingly, countries that were in negotiations were encouraged to complete them and countries that had not yet initiated them were encouraged to do so. Countries were also encouraged to ensure that their bilateral arrangements for effective exchange of information for all civil and criminal tax matters provide benefits for both parties.

8.   As regards collective actions, it was agreed the Global Forum would provide periodic progress reports on developments after the initial report was released. Countries were encouraged to regularly provide updates on developments in their legal and administrative frameworks with respect to transparency and effective exchange of information and that information will be made available to all participants. The 2006

---

[5] See paragraph 14(i) of The Gleneagles Communiqué on Africa, July 14, 2005.

[6] See G-20 Statement on Transparency and Exchange of Information for Tax Purposes, Berlin November 2004. (Full Text available at www.oecd.org/ctp/eoi).

[7] See Progress Towards a Level Playing Field: Outcomes of the OECD Global Forum on Taxation (hereafter referred to as the Statement of Outcomes) (Annex II).

[8] See paragraph 8 of the Statement of Outcomes.

Report and its updates are expected to play an important role as an ongoing reference tool and as a tool to assess transparency and the effective exchange of information in tax matters.[9]

9.   This report contains the first such update of the information in the 2006 Report. It reflects participants' legal and administrative frameworks as of 1 January 2007.

10.   In order to prepare this report, participants were asked to review and update the tables in Annex IV of the 2006 Report to ensure they portrayed the correct information on their country as of 1 January 2007. In the event that changes were required, participants were asked to provide details of each change, together with an explanation for the change. All of the changes notified were made available to the countries covered by the report, which then had an opportunity to make comments and raise questions. These questions were then forwarded to the relevant country for its consideration.

11.   The tables in Annex IV of the 2006 Report have been revised to reflect the changes reported by countries covered by the report. These tables are contained in Annex III to this report. The countries covered were given an opportunity to review and correct the report and tables and revisions were made based on the comments received.

12.   The remainder of this report is divided into two parts: Part II (Update on Progress) and Part III (Outcomes of Review).

---

[9] See paragraph 22 of the Statement of Outcomes.

II. Update on Progress

13.   This part of the report highlights the main changes made to the information contained in the 2006 Report.

A.   *Exchanging Information*

14.   This section outlines the main changes made to the information on exchange of information contained in tables **A1-A5**.

1.   Existence of Mechanisms for Exchange of Information Upon Request

15.   Table **A1** shows the number of double taxation conventions (DTCs) and tax information exchange agreements (TIEAs) by country. It includes both bilateral and multilateral agreements (e.g. the Caricom Agreement) and indicates the number of agreements under negotiation where countries have disclosed such negotiations. Since 31 December 2005, 86 new DTCs have entered into force in the 82 countries covered by the 2006 Report, resulting in a total of 1814 DTCs in force in these countries. Moreover, the number of bilateral tax information exchange agreements (TIEAs) in force has increased from 46 to 54. The new TIEAs signed since 1 January 2007 between Antigua and Barbuda and Australia, Jersey and the Netherlands and between the Netherlands Antilles and Australia and New Zealand are not included in Table A1. Other countries that reported having few exchange of information mechanisms in the 2006 Report have also increased the number of agreements they have signed or which they are negotiating. For instance, Bermuda now has 7 agreements signed or under negotiation compared to 4 in 2006. San Marino has reported having 4 DTCs in force and 7 that are signed or under negotiation compared to 3 signed agreements in 2006 and 6 signed or under negotiation. There are still 10 countries without TIEAs or DTCs (either in force or signed) that were not engaged in active negotiations at 1 January 2007 (Andorra, Anguilla, Gibraltar, Liechtenstein,[10] Nauru, Niue, Panama, Samoa, Turks and Caicos Islands and Vanuatu).[11] However, a number of these jurisdictions have reported commencing negotiations since 1 January 2007.

16.   Table **A2** shows the countries that have domestic laws that permit some type of information exchange for tax purposes with a brief description of the type of law. Since the publication of the 2006 Report, Australia has enacted new anti-money laundering legislation (the Anti-Money Laundering and Counter-Terrorism Financing Act 2006) which allows for exchange of information in criminal tax matters under the legislative powers of the Australian tax authority, e.g. where a bilateral treaty with respect to exchange of information exists. In Samoa, legislation was submitted to Parliament in 2006 on Mutual Legal Assistance in Criminal Matters, Money Laundering Prevention and Proceeds of Crime which will allow Samoa to obtain information for exchange of information purposes in a much broader range of criminal tax matters. That legislation has now been passed into law but did not come into force until after 1 January 2007.

---

[10]Liechtenstein has DTCs in force with Austria and Switzerland which provide for exchange of information in certain narrow circumstances.

[11] Nothing in this report comments on the ability of a dependency or territory to enter into international treaties.

2. *Scope of Information Exchange*

17.   Table **A3** shows the number of DTCs and TIEAs that provide for information exchange upon request. It includes both bilateral and multilateral agreements (*e.g.* the Caricom Agreement, the Joint Council of Europe/OECD Convention on Mutual Administrative Assistance in Tax Matters and the Nordic Convention on Mutual Assistance). Columns 3 and 4 of the table show by country the number of DTCs and TIEAs with broad and with limited exchange clauses. Since 2006, the number of exchange of information arrangements reported with broad exchange clauses has increased by 90 and the number with limited exchange clauses has decreased by 4. There are now 1606 DTCs that permit information exchange for the administration and enforcement of domestic tax laws ("broad exchange clause") and 208 DTCs that are limited to information necessary for ensuring the correct application of the convention ("limited exchange clause").

18.   The 2006 Report showed that with the exception of 2 agreements, all DTCs that cover information exchange for the application of domestic tax laws (*i.e.* those with a "broad exchange clause") permit information to be exchanged without regard to whether the case, audit or investigation giving rise to a request is classified as a civil or a criminal tax matter. The two exceptions were the DTCs between Switzerland and the United States and between Switzerland and Germany. In the past, Switzerland had provided information in the application of domestic criminal tax laws only through mechanisms of legal assistance (mutual legal assistance treaties and domestic law). Following the renegotiation of its treaty with the United States in 1997 and its undertaking in connection with the 2000 OECD Report, *Improving Access to Bank Information for Tax Purposes*, Switzerland is now willing to broaden the scope of its DTCs and has already done so in connection with its DTC with Germany. The 2006 Report reflected that Switzerland's DTCs with the United States and Germany were the only two Swiss DTCs that covered exchange of information for purposes of the administration or enforcement of domestic tax law (*i.e.* they have a broad exchange clause, although limited to assistance in the area of criminal tax matters). Since then, protocols to the DTCs between Finland and Switzerland and Norway and Switzerland have been signed and are now in force, which produce the same result as the treaties with Germany and the United States. In addition, Switzerland has initialled a protocol to its DTC with the United Kingdom, and has signed protocols to its bilateral conventions with Austria and Spain that provide for the exchange of information upon request in cases of tax fraud and the like. The revisions of the treaties with Austria, Finland, Norway, Spain and the United Kingdom also provide for another significant departure from Switzerland's previous practice in that they allow for exchange of information in both civil and criminal tax matters for holding companies. Switzerland is engaged in negotiations with other countries to include similar provisions in its treaties with those countries.

19.   Table **A4** is a summary of all the mechanisms that permit information exchange in tax matters and shows for each country reviewed the number and type of information exchange relationships. An update of the consolidation of all the mechanisms that permit information exchange shows that 70 of the 82 reviewed countries have one or more exchange of information relationships covering all tax matters; 46 countries have one or more exchange relationships covering certain civil tax matters, and 80 countries have one or more exchange of information relationships covering, at least certain criminal tax matters.

3.   Dual Criminality and Domestic Tax Interest

20.   In the 2006 Report, it was reported that the United Kingdom does not require a domestic tax interest to exchange information in tax matters provided there is a suitable provision to this effect in the relevant DTC or TIEA in force. In addition, the United Kingdom has been providing information to the other EU Member States without requiring a domestic tax interest under national law implementing the EU Mutual Assistance Directive.[12] The United Kingdom has amended its domestic law (in the Finance Act 2006) to remove the domestic tax interest requirement even in relation to the bilateral tax treaties that do not include an express provision to eliminate it. This leaves only 5 countries (Cyprus,[13] Hong Kong, China; Malaysia; Philippines and Singapore) that require the information to be relevant for domestic tax purposes in order to respond to a request for information pursuant to DTCs and TIEAs.

21.   Table **A5** shows the application of the dual criminality principle in all countries reviewed that restrict information exchange on request for the application or enforcement of the domestic tax law of the requesting country to criminal tax matters. It also provides a general understanding of the standard of criminality that applies. The only change in this table is the deletion of the entries for Switzerland. As explained in paragraph 18, Switzerland now has mechanisms in place that permit the exchange of information in civil tax matters in the case of holding companies.

B.   Access to Bank Information

22.   This section outlines the main changes made to the information on access to bank information contained in tables **B1-B3**.

1.   Bank Secrecy Rules

23.   In all of the countries reviewed, banks are required to treat their customers' affairs as confidential or secret towards ordinary third parties. Table **B1** shows for all countries reviewed whether the basis for bank secrecy arises purely out of the relationship between the bank and its customer (*e.g.* contract, common law) or whether it has been reinforced by statute. It further shows whether statutory provisions are limited to particular customers or market segments or whether they are of general application. The table does not deal with bank secrecy towards tax authorities which is addressed in Table **B2**. There have been no changes made to Table **B1**.

2.   Access to Bank Information for Tax Purposes

24.   Table **B2** shows the extent to which countries reviewed have access to bank information for exchange of information purposes.

---

[12]Council Directive 77/799/EEC of 19 December 1977 concerning mutual assistance by the competent authorities of the Member States in the field of direct taxation, certain excise duties and taxation of insurance premiums.

[13]   - Note by Turkey:
The information in this document with reference to « Cyprus » relates to the southern part of the Island. There is no single authority representing both Turkish and Greek Cypriot people on the Island. Turkey recognizes the Turkish Republic of Northern Cyprus (TRNC). Until a lasting and equitable solution is found within the context of United Nations, Turkey shall preserve its position concerning the "Cyprus issue".
   - Note by all the European Union Member States of the OECD and the European Commission:
The Republic of Cyprus is recognized by all members of the United Nations with the exception of Turkey. The information in this document relates to the area under the effective control of the Government of the Republic of Cyprus.

25.   As noted in the 2006 Report, in Belgium the tax authorities have access to bank information for civil tax purposes if an audit reveals specific elements which allow the tax authorities to presume the existence, or the preparation, of a tax fraud. Further, in the case of an administrative appeal, the tax authorities have access to bank information if the taxpayer refuses to provide it. On 27 November 2006, Belgium and the United States signed a DTC which provides for exchange of bank information, upon request. The exchange of information article states that, in order to obtain bank information, the tax administration of the requested Contracting State shall have the power to ask for the disclosure of information and to conduct investigations and hearings notwithstanding any contrary provisions in its domestic tax laws. Under the law which approves the DTC, the Belgian tax administration is authorised to obtain from banks the information requested by the United States' competent authority on the basis of the DTC. Further, Belgium has stated its openness to negotiate bilaterally exchange of information on bank information with other countries.

26.   Bahrain has enacted new legislation (Law No. 64 of 2006, with respect to promulgating the Central Bank of Bahrain and Financial Institutions Law) which provides that Bahrain may obtain information not only from banks but also from other financial institutions.

27.   Jersey has enacted legislation which enables it to obtain bank and other information for the purposes of its TIEA with the United States. Equivalent legislative provisions will be enacted for the purposes of other TIEAs as and when they are concluded.

3.   *Specificity Required and Powers to Obtain and Compel Information in the Case of Refusal to Cooperate*

28.   Table **B3** shows for each of the countries reviewed whether the country's competent authority has the power to obtain bank information directly or if separate authorisation is required. It also indicates whether a country has measures in place to compel the production of information if a bank refuses to provide information to the country's authorities. There have been no significant changes made to the table.

C.   *Access to Ownership, Identity and Accounting Information*

29.   This section outlines the main changes made to tables **C1-C3** relating to availability of reliable information (in particular ownership, identity and accounting information) and powers to obtain and provide such information in response to a specific request.

1.   *Information Gathering Powers*

30.   Table **C1** gives an overview of the information gathering powers available to the authorities in each of the countries reviewed to obtain information in response to a request for exchange of information for tax purposes. A total of 78 of the 82 countries reviewed generally have powers to obtain information that is kept by a person subject to record keeping obligations which may be invoked to respond to a request for exchange of information. Of these, 67 countries may obtain information in both criminal and civil tax matters to respond to a request for exchange of information. This includes Guernsey and Jersey both of which have now enacted new legislation to enable them to obtain information in civil tax matters for exchange of information purposes. In addition, 71 of the 82 countries reviewed have reported that they also generally have powers to obtain information from persons not required to keep such information which may be invoked to

respond to a request for information. Of these, 58 countries have reported that they can obtain information to respond to a request in both criminal and civil tax matters. Guatemala and Nauru still have no powers at all to obtain information for exchange of information purposes.

2.   *Specific Secrecy Provisions*

31.   Table **C2** shows the countries that have specific confidentiality or secrecy provisions relating to the disclosure of ownership, identity or accounting information. Where such provisions exist, the table indicates whether the provisions are of a general or a specific nature and whether they are overridden if a request is made pursuant to an exchange of information arrangement. In the 2006 Report, Bahrain was reported as one of the two countries (the other being Monaco) having no trust law but having special provisions for trusts formed under foreign law. The update shows that in 2006, a new statutory law to govern trustees and trust administration (the 2006 Financial Trust Law) was enacted in Bahrain. Under this law a trustee must not disclose to a third party, any accounts or data or information, or deliver any documents relating to the trust, except as provided by law, or required by agreement or by the nature of the transaction relating to the trust, or imposed by an order issued by a competent court or by the Dispute Resolution Committee. The Central Bank of Bahrain, however, has the right to question the trustee who must allow it to access the accounts, documents and records of the trust. The Central Bank can access information so held under the Financial Trust Law if a properly made request for information is submitted pursuant to a treaty. In addition, the update shows that Samoa's statutory confidentiality or secrecy provisions are overridden if a request for information is made pursuant to an exchange of information arrangement. Singapore has also clarified that confidentiality provisions specific to trust companies may be overridden in connection with a request for exchange of information made under the Mutual Assistance in Criminal Matters Act or under a DTC where Singapore has a domestic tax interest. This means that 34 of the 82 countries reviewed have specific confidentiality or secrecy provisions relating to the disclosure of ownership, identity or accounting information. In 25 of these cases, the confidentiality provisions can in certain circumstances be overridden or do not apply where information is requested for the purpose of responding to a request pursuant to a tax information exchange mechanism.

3.   *Bearer Securities*

32.   Table **C3** shows which of the countries reviewed allow for the issuance of bearer shares and bearer debt instruments. Where countries permit the issuance of bearer instruments, the table outlines the measures adopted to identify the owners of such instruments. Macao, China has reported that new anti-money laundering legislation now requires financial institutions to undertake customer due diligence, including identifying the owners of bearer shares. San Marino has reported that a legislative change in 2006 requires that, from 1 January 2008, meetings of joint stock corporations must be held in the presence of a notary public, who is required to identify the holder of bearer shares and retain that information for five years. Hong Kong, China and the Slovak Republic have clarified the information previously reported as to bearer shares and bearer debt instruments. Bearer shares may be issued in Hong Kong, China, which also has mechanisms to identify the owners of such shares in some cases. Bearer shares and bearer debt instruments can be issued in the Slovak Republic, but there are mechanisms to identify owners of both bearer shares and bearer debt instruments. Thus, the update shows that 49 countries permit the issuance of bearer shares and that 53 permit the issuance of bearer debt instruments.

Further, a total of 41 countries have adopted mechanisms to identify the legal owners of bearer shares in some or all cases and 42 countries have adopted mechanisms to identify the owners of bearer debt instruments.

D.   Availability of Ownership, Identity and Accounting Information

1.   Ownership Information

33.   This section outlines the main changes made in tables **D1-D5** regarding the availability of ownership and identity information on companies, trusts, partnerships, foundations and other relevant organisational structures.

34.   Table **D1** shows, in relation to companies in each of the reviewed countries, the type of ownership information required to be held by governmental authorities, at the company level and by service providers.[14]   Since the publication of the 2006 Report, Macao, China has enacted new anti-money laundering legislation and established a new administrative framework which requires financial institutions to verify the identity of new customers and their beneficial owners. Moreover, Aruba and Hong Kong, China have clarified that, under their anti-money laundering legislation, financial institutions are required to verify the identity of customers and their beneficial owners. In Aruba, legislation has also been submitted to Parliament that will extend customer identification and record keeping requirements to corporate service providers. Singapore has also clarified that there are requirements in Singapore for service providers to hold ownership information. Singapore has anti-money laundering and combating financing of terrorism legislation and guidelines that apply to financial, legal and accounting service providers which require them to conduct customer due diligence. Further, the update shows that publicly listed companies in Singapore are required to keep a register of "substantial shareholders" (persons having legal, beneficial or deemed interests in 5 % or more of voting shares). Thus, all but one of the countries reviewed (Guatemala) have now indicated that, where applicable, anti-money laundering legislation would normally require corporate or other service providers to identify the beneficial owners of their client companies. In the Isle of Man, a new Companies Act was passed in October 2006. Companies incorporated under the new Act are required at all times to have a registered agent in the Isle of Man. A registered agent must hold a licence under the Fiduciary Services Acts and is responsible for maintaining various records and information including details of legal and beneficial ownership.

35.   Table **D2** shows which countries have domestic trust laws or separate domestic trust laws that apply only to non-resident settlors and beneficiaries; and which countries without trust laws allow their residents to act as trustees of foreign trusts. In the 2006 Report, Bahrain was reported as being one of the two countries (the other being Monaco) with no trust law that have special provisions for trusts formed under foreign law. The update shows that in 2006, a new statutory domestic trust law (the 2006 Financial Trust Law) was enacted in Bahrain, in order to govern trustees and trust administration. Thus, 55 of the 82 countries reviewed now have trust laws.

36.   Table **D3** shows, in relation to trusts in each of the countries covered, the type of identity information (on settlors and beneficiaries of trusts) required to be held by governmental authorities, resident trustees of a domestic trust or a foreign trust and service

---

[14]References to service providers in this report and in the annexes of the report include banks, corporate service providers and other persons.

providers. In Bahrain, under the 2006 Financial Trust Law, information on the identity of settlors and beneficiaries is required to be held by both a governmental authority and by the trustee. Service providers are required to keep information under trust law as well as under the anti-money laundering legislation. In the United Arab Emirates, since 23 January 2007 rules issued by the Dubai Financial Services Authority relating to the regulation of Trust Service Providers provide that such service providers must at all times have verified documentary evidence of the settlors, trustees, beneficiaries and any person entitled to receive a distribution.

37.   Table **D4** shows the type of identity information required to be held, in respect of partnerships, by governmental authorities, at the partnership level and by service providers. The United Arab Emirates has enacted a new Limited Partnership Law which provides for the same identity disclosure requirements as under the Limited Liability Partnership Law. Since Singapore has reported that its anti-money laundering legislation requires service providers to keep identity information on partners, it follows that this requirement now applies in 52 of the countries reviewed.

38.   Table **D5** shows the type of identity information required to be held in respect of foundations (founders, beneficiaries and members of foundation councils) by governmental authorities, at the foundation level and by service providers. The table has been amended to reflect the new anti-money laundering framework in Macao, China and the enactment in Saint Kitts & Nevis of legislation on foundations.[15]

2.   *Accounting Information*

39.   This section outlines the main changes made in tables **D6-D9** on the availability and reliability of accounting records.

40.   Table **D6** shows, in respect of companies in each of the countries covered, the requirements relating to the nature of the accounting records that must be created and retained, specific requirements with respect to their auditing and filing with a governmental authority and the rules regarding the retention of the records. In the Isle of Man, companies incorporated under the new Companies Act 2006 are required to keep reliable accounting records at the office of the registered agent. These companies are not required to be audited. Other than that, there have been no significant changes made to this table.

41.   Table **D7** describes the requirements to keep accounting information in relation to trusts in the countries reported as having domestic trust laws. Since Bahrain enacted the 2006 Financial Trust Law last year, there is now a requirement to keep accounting records under domestic trust law instead of the Financial Trust Regulation. Guernsey has enacted new legislation requiring trustees that receive business income or income from the letting of property subject to Guernsey tax to maintain detailed records for tax purposes. Similar requirements apply to partnerships. In Japan, following an amendment of the trust law in 2006, trustees now have the obligation to keep and store books and records. The accounting records must be sufficient to show and explain all the trust's transactions and calculations. Other than that, there have been no significant changes made to this table.

42.   Table **D8** describes the requirements to keep accounting information on partnerships in each of the countries covered. There have been no significant changes made to this table apart from the change referred to in paragraph 41, above, in relation to Guernsey.

---

[15] Only with respect to Nevis.

43.   Table **D9** shows the requirements to keep accounting information relating to foundations. In Saint Kitts & Nevis, foundations established under the Nevis Multiform Foundation Ordinance are required to keep accounting records in all cases. In Switzerland, a new law entered into force on 1 January 2006 (modification of the Swiss Civil Code, Art. 84b) providing for a general obligation to keep accounting records and not only for foundations engaged in a commercial activity. Other than that, there have been no significant changes made to this table.

III.   Outcomes of Review

44.   This update report covers the legal and administrative frameworks in relation to transparency and exchange of information for tax purposes in 82 countries. The update indicates that:

- 80 of the countries covered have legal mechanisms in place to exchange information in criminal tax matters in certain circumstances.

- Following certain changes in Switzerland's treaty policy, only 3[16] countries continue to apply the principle of dual incrimination to all of their information exchange relationships.

- 70 of the countries covered have legal mechanisms in place that permit exchange of information for both civil and criminal tax matters.

- There remain 11[17] countries that do not have tax information exchange agreements in the form of DTCs or TIEAs that are either signed or in force.

- Of the countries that are able to exchange information for both civil and criminal tax matters, 5[18] still report being unable to respond to a request for exchange of information where they have no interest in obtaining the information for their own tax purposes (domestic tax interest). As a result of changes in its domestic tax law, the United Kingdom, no longer requires a domestic tax interest to exchange information under any of its DTCs.

- 77 of the countries covered in the update are able to obtain and provide banking information in response to a request for information in criminal tax matters in some or all cases.

- 50 of the countries covered are able to obtain and provide banking information in response to a request for information related to a civil tax matter in all cases. A further 10[19] countries have access to bank information for exchange purposes in certain civil tax matters while 17[20] countries only have access to bank information for the purposes of responding to a request for exchange of information in criminal tax matters.

- There remain 3[21] countries that are unable to obtain access to bank information for any tax information exchange purpose.

---

[16] Andorra, Cook Islands and Samoa.

[17] Andorra, Anguilla, Cook Islands, Gibraltar, Liechtenstein, Nauru, Niue, Panama, Samoa, Turks and Caicos Islands and Vanuatu.

[18] Cyprus; Hong Kong, China; Malaysia; Philippines and Singapore.

[19] Anguilla; Belgium; Cyprus; Gibraltar; Hong Kong, China; Malaysia; Malta; Montserrat; Philippines and Singapore.

[20] Andorra; Austria; Belize; Cook Islands; Liechtenstein; Luxembourg; Macao, China; Niue; Samoa; San Marino; Saint Kitts and Nevis; Saint Lucia; Saint Vincent and the Grenadines; Switzerland; Turks and Caicos Islands; Uruguay and Vanuatu. With respect to 2 of the countries (Brunei and Dominica) there is insufficient information to make an assessment concerning their ability to access bank information for exchange of information purposes.

[21] Guatemala, Nauru and Panama.

- 78 countries reported having the power to obtain information, for at least some information exchange purposes, where such information is required to be kept for tax or other purposes.

- 11[22] countries are able to obtain information only where the request relates to a criminal tax matter.

- 77 countries reported that information on legal ownership for all companies (other than for bearer shares) is held either by a governmental authority or the company itself. Further, all but one country (Guatemala) reported that, where applicable, anti-money legislation would require service providers to identify the beneficial owners of companies.

- 49 countries permit the issuance of bearer shares and all but 8 of these reported having mechanisms to identify the owners of such shares in some or all cases.

- 55 of the countries reviewed have a domestic trust law of which 50 reported that information on the identity of settlors and beneficiaries is required to be held under their laws either by a governmental authority, the trustees or by a service provider or other person.

- Of the 68 countries that have partnership laws, 46 countries reported that identity information is held by a governmental authority with respect to partnerships in all cases.

- With respect to accounting information, 75 countries require accounting information to be maintained by all companies. Of the 55 countries that have a domestic trust law, 46 reported requiring all trusts formed under their law to keep accounting records.

45. This report shows that incremental progress continues to be made towards implementing the standards that the Global Forum wishes to see achieved. There is now a greater number of exchange arrangements in place than a year ago and the scope of some existing arrangements, such as those of Switzerland, have been extended. In the United Kingdom, a domestic tax interest requirement is no longer invoked in any situation. Some countries have also improved their capacity to exchange information in criminal tax matters or are in the process of doing so. Access to bank and ownership information has also been greatly improved in Belgium and Bahrain. Enhanced record keeping requirements have been introduced in some countries (e.g. Isle of Man, Japan and San Marino). Others such as Guernsey and Jersey, have brought into force new legislation to provide them with the powers necessary to fully implement the provisions of their bilateral exchange of information arrangements. Thus, the trend towards the implementation of the high standards of transparency and exchange of information established by the Global Forum continues.

---

[22] Andorra, Anguilla, Cook Islands, Liechtenstein, Montserrat, Niue, Panama, Samoa, Saint Vincent and the Grenadines, Turks and Caicos Islands and Vanuatu.

Annex I:
Countries Covered by Factual Assessment and Included in the Tables

Global Forum Participating Partners

Anguilla*	Dominica	Korea	San Marino
Antigua and Barbuda	Finland	Malta	Seychelles
Aruba**	France	Mauritius	Slovak Republic
Australia	Germany	Mexico	Spain
The Bahamas	Gibraltar*	Montserrat*	Saint Kitts and Nevis
Bahrain, Kingdom of	Greece	Nauru	Saint Lucia
Belize	Grenada	Netherlands**	Saint Vincent and The Grenadines
Bermuda*	Guernsey***	Netherlands Antilles**	Sweden
British Virgin Islands*	Hungary	New Zealand	Turkey
Canada	Iceland	Niue	Turks and Caicos Islands*
Cayman Islands*	Ireland	Norway	United Kingdom
Cook Islands	Isle of Man***	Panama	United States
Cyprus	Italy	Poland	U. S. Virgin Islands****
Czech Republic	Japan	Portugal	Vanuatu
Denmark	Jersey***	Samoa	

* Overseas Territory of the United Kingdom
** The Netherlands, the Netherlands Antilles and Aruba are the three countries of the Kingdom of the Netherlands
*** Dependency of the British Crown
**** External Territory of the United States

Other Countries[23]

Andorra	Guatemala	Philippines
Argentina	**Hong Kong, China**	**Russian Federation**
Austria	Liechtenstein	Singapore
Barbados	Luxembourg	**South Africa**
Belgium	**Macao, China**	Switzerland
Brunei	Malaysia	**United Arab Emirates**
China	Marshall Islands	Uruguay
Costa Rica	Monaco	

---

[23] The countries in bold have endorsed the principles of transparency and effective exchange of information in tax matters. See paragraph 4 supra.

Annex II:
Progress Towards a Level Playing Field:
Outcomes of the OECD Global Forum on Taxation
Melbourne, 15-16 November 2005

Over 130 representatives of 55 governments, the Commonwealth Secretariat and the European Commission met on 15-16 November 2005 in Melbourne to review progress towards a level playing field based on high standards of transparency and effective exchange of information for tax purposes. The meeting was chaired by Mr. Papali'i Tommy Scanlan, Governor of the Central Bank of Samoa and Mr. Bill McCloskey, Chair of the OECD's Committee on Fiscal Affairs. Mr. Peter Costello, MP, Treasurer of the Commonwealth of Australia, opened the meeting.

The two day discussions, which were based upon the review of the legal and administrative frameworks on transparency and exchange of information in tax matters currently in place in over 80 countries, showed that considerable progress has already been made towards a global level playing field in the areas of transparency and effective exchange of information in tax matters. The discussions identified a number of areas where further progress needs to be made. The review will be published early in 2006.

The attached statement sets out the outcomes from the two day meeting as well as the next steps in the process.

A. Introduction and Background

1.   On 15-16 November 2005, Australia hosted the fourth meeting of the OECD Global Forum on Taxation[1] to discuss the importance of achieving a global level playing field[2] in

---

[1] The OECD carries out its dialogue on tax issues with non-OECD economies under the multilateral framework known as the "Global Forum on Taxation". The composition of the Global Forum generally varies depending on the topics covered by the meeting.

[2] The global level playing field concept, features and role is defined in paragraph 6 of the Berlin Report as follows:

A) CONCEPT:

The level playing field is fundamentally about fairness to which all parties in the Global Forum are committed.

In the context of exchange of information achieving a level playing field means the convergence of existing practices to the same high standards for effective exchange of information on both criminal and civil taxation matters within an acceptable timeline for implementation with the aim of achieving equity and fair competition.

B) FEATURES:

Will provide for –

i)   inclusive process
ii)   mutual benefits through bilateral implementation
iii)   a consistent and rigorous approach to any failure to implement
iv)   review and verification mechanisms
v)   the standard and the timeline.

respect of improving transparency and effective exchange of information in the tax area. Over 130 representatives from 55 governments met in Melbourne to review progress towards a level playing field in these areas. The meeting was chaired by Mr. Papali'i Tommy Scanlan, Governor of the Central Bank of Samoa, and Bill McCloskey, Chair of the OECD's Committee on Fiscal Affairs. The Honourable Peter Costello, MP, Treasurer of the Commonwealth of Australia, opened the meeting.

2.   The purpose of the Melbourne meeting was to review implementation of the process agreed at the Global Forum meeting held in Berlin in June 2004 for working towards a global level playing field based on high standards of transparency and effective exchange of information in tax matters. Two key aspects of this process were to invite other significant financial centres to participate in the dialogue and to carry out a review of countries' (which included the Invitees)[3] legal and administrative frameworks in the areas of transparency and exchange of information in tax matters. A draft report of the results of the review was circulated to all participants and formed the basis of the Global Forum's discussions (hereafter referred to as the "Draft Report"). The Draft Report was prepared on the basis of information gathered using a template/questionnaire.

3.   The Melbourne Global Forum Participating Partners welcomed representatives from a number of countries that were attending for the first time as Invitees to the Global Forum's dialogue on transparency and effective exchange of information in tax matters.[4]

B. The Review of Countries' Legal and Administrative Frameworks

4.   81 countries were included in the review of their legal and administrative frameworks initiated at the 2004 Berlin Global Forum meeting and the discussions at the Melbourne meeting reveal that progress is being made towards a level playing field in the areas of transparency and effective exchange of information in tax matters. The review of the template information (the "review") carried out at the Melbourne meeting suggests that on the information currently available:

- 80 of the countries reviewed reported having legal mechanisms in place to permit the exchange of information in criminal tax matters in certain circumstances.

- 65 of the countries reviewed have legal mechanisms in place that permit the exchange of information for both criminal and civil tax matters.

C) ROLE:

The level playing field serves as a goal.

Achieving a level playing field in respect of exchange of information requires that all jurisdictions, OECD and non-OECD members, should act in a manner consistent with the concept in their bilateral relationships and more broadly.

[3] References in this document to "countries" should be taken to apply equally to "territories", "dependent territories" or "jurisdictions".

[4] In the context of the Melbourne Global Forum meeting and of this paper, the term "Global Forum" is understood as the grouping of OECD and non-OECD economies that have agreed to work together towards a level playing field in the areas of transparency and exchange of information in tax matters. These economies are referred to as Participating Partners. The Global Forum agreed at its 2004 meeting to invite other economies to the Melbourne meeting. See Appendix. Not all the views expressed in this paper are shared by all of the Invitees.

- Of the countries that are able to exchange information for both civil and criminal tax purposes, the vast majority do not require a domestic tax interest to obtain and respond to a request for information.

- 73 of the countries reviewed are able to obtain and provide banking information in response to a request for information related to a criminal tax matter in some or all cases.

- 53 of the countries reviewed are able to obtain and provide banking information in response to a request for information related to a civil tax matter in some or all cases.

- All countries that are able to exchange information reported having safeguards in place to protect the confidentiality of any information exchanged.

- 74 of the countries reviewed reported that ownership information is available for companies and 45 countries reported it was available with respect to partnerships. In most cases, legal ownership information is available. Beneficial ownership information is available in an increasing number of countries.

- 74 of the countries reviewed require accounting information to be maintained by or for companies. Of the 53 countries that have trust law, 43 require trusts to keep accounting records.

5.   The review undertaken suggests that both OECD and non-OECD countries have implemented or made considerable progress towards implementing many of the transparency and effective exchange of information standards that the Global Forum wishes to see achieved. There is no longer any OECD country where a domestic tax interest, of itself, is an impediment to exchange of information. A growing number of non-OECD economies are negotiating agreements that provide for exchange of information[5] many countries have improved transparency by implementing the FATF customer due diligence requirements and several countries have recently required bearer shares to be immobilised or held by an approved custodian (*e.g.* the British Virgin Islands, the Cook Islands, Saint Kitts and Nevis). The Global Forum welcomes these developments but further progress is needed if a global level playing field is to be achieved. The remainder of this note discusses possible next steps in the Global Forum's work.

C. Next Steps

6.   It is useful to consider the next steps in terms of the categories of actions that formed the basis of the process established in Berlin. The process endorsed at the Berlin Global Forum meeting recognised that integrated individual, bilateral and collective actions would be needed both to achieve and to maintain the goal of a level playing field.

(i) Individual actions

7.   In terms of *individual actions*, the Berlin Report referred to the fact that some countries may need to modify some existing laws and practices to fully implement the principles of transparency and effective exchange of information in tax matters. Despite

---

[5] For example, Aruba, Bahrain, Bermuda, British Virgin Islands, Cayman Islands, Guernsey, Jersey, Isle of Man, Mauritius, the Netherlands Antilles and the Seychelles.

the progress referred to in the previous section, further actions at the individual country level remain necessary.

8.   The Global Forum recognised that countries will not be able to move simultaneously to make the necessary changes due to differences in legal systems and in the issues – political, economic and institutional -- that different countries would need to address. Nevertheless, all countries are strongly encouraged to take the necessary steps towards a level playing field. In particular:

  i.   Further progress is required in some countries to address the constraints placed on international co-operation to counter criminal tax abuses. In today's global environment it is important for all countries to co-operate with other countries in the fight against all financial crimes, including tax crimes, and this requires the implementation of transparency and the establishment of effective exchange of information mechanisms. The small number of countries that have such constraints on their ability to co-operate in fighting tax crimes are encouraged to review their current policies and to report the outcome of their review at the next Global Forum meeting.

  ii. Further progress is required to address those instances where countries require a domestic tax interest to obtain and provide information in response to a specific request for information related to a tax matter. Those countries where this is still a requirement are encouraged to review their current policies on this issue and to report the outcome of their review at the next Global Forum meeting.

  iii. Further progress is required in the area of access to bank information for tax purposes. Although most countries reported being able to obtain such information for criminal tax matters, a number of countries continue to have strict limits on access to bank information which excessively constrain their ability to respond to specific requests for information in civil and criminal tax cases. Those countries are encouraged to review their current policies on this issue and to report the outcome of their review at the next Global Forum meeting.

  iv. Further progress is required in some countries to ensure that competent authorities have appropriate powers to obtain information for civil and criminal tax purposes. Although the majority of countries have such powers some countries reported limitations on the use of their information-gathering powers to the onshore sector or otherwise lack the power to obtain information for exchange of information purposes. Those countries are encouraged to review their current policies and to report the outcome of their review at the next Global Forum meeting.

  v.   Most countries have access to legal ownership information of companies, trusts, partnerships, foundations and other organisational structures. Beneficial ownership information is available in a far fewer, but an increasing, number of countries. Further improvement is necessary. A large number of countries still allow bearer shares. In some countries the availability of ownership information is further complicated by the fact that responsibility for corporate law is in the hands of political sub-divisions. Progress in this area is expected to be assisted by countries' implementation of Recommendations 5, 33 and 34 of the FATF Recommendations and other international initiatives (e.g. EU Second and Third

Money Laundering Directives[6]). Countries are encouraged to review their current policies, including those of political subdivisions, if relevant, and to report the outcome of their review at the next Global Forum meeting.

vi. Most countries reviewed reported requiring the keeping of accounts by companies and partnerships. However, certain exceptions to this requirement exist, notably in the context of some international company regimes. Those countries that do not require the keeping of accounting records for international company regimes are encouraged to review their current policies and to report the outcome of their review at the next Global Forum meeting.

9.   The Berlin Report also referred to the important role that individual countries can play in encouraging other countries to implement the principles, including through the use of "other organisations to which they belong, fora in which they participate, and communications with their business communities to encourage the adoption of these practices". Over the last year, several countries did use their participation in other organisations and groups to promote the implementation of the principles of transparency and effective exchange of information. In July 2005, the G-8 Heads of Government endorsed at the Gleneagles Summit the work on transparency and exchange of information and encouraged all countries to implement those principles[7]. The G-20 Finance Ministers and Central Bank Governors issued a statement on 21 November 2004 committing themselves "to the high standards of transparency and exchange of information for tax purposes that have been reflected in the Model Agreement on Exchange of Information on Tax Matters" and "call[ed] on all countries to adopt these standards." They further "strongly support[ed] the efforts of the OECD Global Forum on Taxation to promote high standards of transparency and exchange of information for tax purposes and to provide a cooperative forum in which all countries can work towards the establishment of a level playing field based on these standards."[8] Further actions by such groupings and in other fora could help foster progress towards a level playing field.

10.   The Berlin Report also suggested that countries should develop and implement communications strategies aimed at promoting the principles of transparency and exchange of information for tax purposes to their business communities. Members of the Global Forum have participated in numerous events organised by the financial community and this has helped to promote a better understanding of the objectives of the Global Forum. Ensuring that business understands the objectives of the Global Forum's work and the importance of transparency and effective exchange of information in an increasingly globalised world will make the implementation of these principles more politically acceptable.

11.   Public awareness campaigns are also important in efforts to improve taxpayer compliance. Voluntary compliance with the tax laws is often influenced by the public's

---

[6] The EU Second Money Laundering Directive has been transposed into the domestic law of all EU Member States. The EU Third Money Laundering Directive has been adopted by the Council of Economic and Finance Ministers but has not yet been transposed into the domestic law of the Member States.

[7] See paragraph 14(i) of The Gleneagles Communiqué on Africa, July 14.

[8] The members of the G-20 are the finance ministers and central bank governors of 19 countries: Argentina, Australia, Brazil, Canada, China, France, Germany, India, Indonesia, Italy, Japan, Korea, Mexico, Russia, Saudi-Arabia, South Africa, Turkey, the United Kingdom and the United States. Another member is the European Union, represented by the Council presidency and the President of the European Central Bank. The managing director of the IMF and the president of the World Bank, plus the chairpersons of the International Monetary and Financial Committee and Development Committee of the IMF and World Bank, also participate in the talks as ex-officio members·

perceptions of overall compliance. Until all countries adopt and implement the high standards of transparency and effective exchange of information, there will continue to be a risk that the public will perceive that secure tax evasion opportunities exist abroad. Individual countries can counter such perceptions by publicising their efforts to pursue taxpayers that fail to comply with their tax obligations in their countries of residence by abusing the anonymity offered by some countries. Countries should also publicise that they are entering into bilateral agreements to be able to obtain the information necessary to ensure compliance with the tax laws by all taxpayers.

12.   Individual countries can also pursue acceptance of the principles of transparency and exchange of information by not marketing themselves as places where anonymity from foreign tax authorities is assured and by countering attempts at such marketing or the promotion of structures or arrangements that rely upon anonymity to avoid tax obligations and by encouraging any political subdivisions that do so market themselves to desist from doing so.

(ii) Bilateral actions

13.   In terms of *bilateral actions*, the Berlin Report highlighted that the principle of effective exchange of information for civil and criminal tax matters will generally be implemented through a process of bilateral negotiations. The Berlin Report acknowledged that "[i]t would be ideal if all significant financial centres would agree to and implement high standards of information exchange at the same time and manner" but recognised that because exchange of information is generally implemented on a bilateral basis, there would be some timing differences in implementation. The global level playing field concept as defined in the Berlin Report does, however, incorporate the expectation that bilateral implementation of those standards should be achieved within an acceptable timeframe and not be open-ended so as to ensure fairness and equity of the process.

14.   The Berlin Report pointed out that the bilateral "process permits the contracting parties to take account of the totality of their bilateral relations, their respective legal systems and practices, and their mutual economic interests." The Berlin Report encouraged all countries to strive to achieve effective exchange of information and transparency by 2006 but recognised that countries could adapt their bilateral arrangements to suit their specific needs and mutual interests.

15.   The review of countries' legal and administrative frameworks suggests that the vast majority of countries are already in a position to exchange information in cases of tax crimes. It is important for all countries to participate in the fight against all financial crimes, including tax crimes, and those countries that are not yet able to do so are encouraged to enter into bilateral arrangements for exchanging information with other countries to combat tax crimes. Those countries that currently are able to provide such assistance are encouraged to review their current legal and administrative frameworks with a view to ensuring the widest possible co-operation among countries to combat tax crimes.

16.   The review suggests that most countries reviewed also have laws and legal instruments in place that would enable effective exchange of information for criminal and civil tax purposes. Progress in bilateral negotiations has been made recently by some countries and others are in the process of such negotiations.

17.   An indicator of the developing co-operation between OECD and non-OECD countries is the increase in tax information exchange agreements and double taxation

agreements.[9] Countries that are currently in negotiations are encouraged to complete them and those countries which have not initiated such negotiations are encouraged to do so.

18.   In the vast majority of cases where bilateral arrangements exist for effective exchange of information for both civil and criminal tax matters, including the agreements referred to above, the parties derive mutual benefits from the arrangement either as a result of a likely balance in the exchange of information or through other benefits. Ensuring that mutual benefits are derived by both parties will further the goal of helping financial centres that meet the high standards set for transparency and effective exchange of information in tax matters to be "fully integrated into the international financial system and the global community."[10] Further, it is hoped that by providing mutual benefits, greater progress towards a level playing field will be made. The nature of any such benefits would necessarily depend on the legal systems and particular circumstances of the two parties to the arrangement. Countries are encouraged to try to ensure that their bilateral arrangements for effective exchange of information for all civil and criminal tax matters provide benefits for both parties.

19.   Public recognition is an important benefit to those countries that implement the principles of transparency and effective exchange of information and OECD countries are encouraged to give recognition where such implementation occurs. Such recognition benefits the other country by enhancing its reputation.

(iii) Collective actions

20.   In terms of *collective actions*, the Berlin Report called for a review of countries' legal and administrative frameworks in the areas of transparency and information exchange, an assessment of the convergence of existing practices and the involvement of significant financial centres that are not currently Participating Partners. The initial analysis of the data received is now well advanced and most of the significant financial centres invited to the Global Forum attended the meeting.

21.   Eighty-one countries were included in the review, which was carried out using a detailed template/questionnaire developed by the Global Forum. As foreseen in the Berlin Report, all of the countries included in the review were invited to complete the template/questionnaire. The information gathered through the template/questionnaire has been summarised in the Draft Report, which will be finalised in early 2006. The issuance of the final report will help to provide public recognition to those countries that have implemented the high standards of transparency and effective exchange of information and ensure that current information on countries' legal and administrative frameworks is widely available.

22.   The Global Forum will provide periodic progress reports on developments after the initial report is released. Countries will be encouraged to regularly provide updates on developments in their legal and administrative frameworks with respect to transparency and effective exchange of information and that information will be made available to all

---

[9] As stated in paragraph 6 of the introduction to the Model Agreement on Exchange of Information on Tax Matters, "[T]he Agreement is intended to establish the standard of what constitutes effective exchange of information for the purposes of the OECD's initiative on harmful tax practices. However, the purpose of the agreement is not to prescribe a specific format for how this standard should be achieved. Thus, the Agreement in either of its forms is only one of several ways in which the standard can be implemented. Other instruments, including double taxation agreements may also be used provided both parties agree to do so, given that other instruments are usually wider in scope."

[10] See paragraph 28 of Berlin Report.

participants. The Report and its updates are expected to play an important role as an ongoing reference tool and as a tool to assess transparency and the effective exchange of information in tax matters.

D. Public Recognition

23.   The Global Forum acknowledges that, for political and historical reasons, changes to improve transparency and to establish effective exchange of information are not always easy and that it is important for international bodies to give public recognition when such changes are implemented.

24.   International bodies may wish to consider providing tangible forms of positive recognition, through their work programmes and in public statements, to countries that implement the principles of transparency and effective exchange of information.

E. Relevance of OECD List of Tax Havens Published in 2000

25.   A number of countries have expressed concern at the way in which some countries have used the 2000 OECD list. If a country chooses to use a list of countries derived from the OECD list, it should do so based on the relevant current facts. Thus, progress made in the implementation of the principles of transparency and effective exchange of information in tax matters should be taken into account by such countries and their legislatures. The 2000 OECD list should be seen in its historical context[11] and as an evaluation by OECD member countries at a particular point in time of which countries met the criteria set out in the 1998 Report. More than five years have passed since the publication of the OECD list and positive changes have occurred in individual countries' transparency and exchange of information laws and practices since that time. The Report, once completed and as updated periodically, will provide more up-to-date information. This does not reflect any judgement by the Global Forum on the tax or other policies underlying country lists.

F.   Endorsement of Principles of Transparency and Effective Exchange of Information

26.   The Global Forum welcomed the endorsement by Argentina; China; Hong Kong, China; Macao, China; the Russian Federation and South Africa of the principles of transparency and effective exchange of information in tax matters and their willingness to work towards a level playing field in these areas.

G. Next Meeting of the Global Forum

27.   The Global Forum welcomed the progress made by the Sub-Group on Level Playing Field Issues[12] in carrying out the mandate given to it at the Berlin Global Forum meeting, confirmed that it would wish the Sub-Group to continue its work and complete its

---

[11] The 2000 Report described the list as follows: "this listing is intended to reflect the technical conclusions of the committee only and is not intended to be used as the basis for possible co-ordinated defensive measures".

[12] The Sub-Group members are: Australia, The Bahamas, Cayman Islands, Cook Islands, France, Germany, Ireland, Isle of Man, Italy, Japan, Jersey, Mauritius, Mexico, Panama, Saint Kitts and Nevis, Samoa, Seychelles and the United States. The Commonwealth Secretariat is an observer.

mandate and agreed that the Sub-Group should propose a date for the next meeting of the Global Forum at which the further progress made on the items discussed in Melbourne would also be addressed.

Appendix to the
Outcomes of the OECD Global Forum on Taxation

Global Forum Participating Partners

Anguilla*	Dominica	Korea	San Marino
Antigua and Barbuda	Finland	Malta	Seychelles
Aruba**	France	Mauritius	Slovak Republic
Australia	Germany	Mexico	Spain
The Bahamas	Gibraltar*	Montserrat*	Saint Kitts and Nevis
Bahrain, Kingdom of	Greece	Nauru	Saint Lucia
Belize	Grenada	Netherlands**	Saint Vincent and The Grenadines
Bermuda*	Guernsey***	Netherlands Antilles**	Sweden
British Virgin Islands*	Hungary	New Zealand	Turkey
Canada	Iceland	Niue	Turks and Caicos Islands*
Cayman Islands*	Ireland	Norway	United Kingdom
Cook Islands	Isle of Man***	Panama	United States
Cyprus	Italy	Poland	U. S. Virgin Islands****
Czech Republic	Japan	Portugal	Vanuatu
Denmark	Jersey***	Samoa	

*   Overseas Territory of the United Kingdom

**   The Netherlands, the Netherlands Antilles and Aruba are the three countries of the Kingdom of the Netherlands

***   Dependency of the British Crown

****   External Territory of the United States

Invitees

In addition to the Participating Partners, set out above, the following countries were invited to contribute to the factual assessment and to attend the Global Forum meeting. The countries in **bold** also attended the Melbourne meeting.

Andorra	Guatemala	**Monaco**
Argentina	**Hong Kong, China**	Philippines
Austria	**Liberia**	Russian Federation
Barbados	Liechtenstein	**Singapore**
Belgium	Luxembourg	**South Africa**
Brunei	**Macao, China**	**Switzerland**
China	**Malaysia**	United Arab Emirates
Costa Rica	Marshall Islands	Uruguay

Annex III:
Country Tables

A.   Exchanging Information

Table A.1.
Number of Double Taxation Conventions and Tax Information Exchange Agreements

Table A1 shows the number of DTCs and TIEAs that provide for exchange of information on request, by country.

The first number shows all DTCs and TIEAs in force. It includes multilateral agreements which are counted as a series of bilateral agreements and the number therefore reflects the number of bilateral exchange relationships created (e.g. the Caricom Agreement is counted as 10 DTCs because it permits each party to exchange information with 10 counterparties).

The second number (in parenthesis) shows the number of agreements not in force but signed or under negotiation where the country has chosen to provide such information. Note that some countries have provided no information on this point, others have reported negotiations with respect to both TIEAs and DTCs and others have limited their comments to TIEA negotiations. The number should therefore be seen in this context. This chart only includes DTCs and TIEAs that allow for information exchange upon request.

Note that exchange of information for tax purposes in the U.S. Virgin Islands is carried out through the U.S. treaty network.

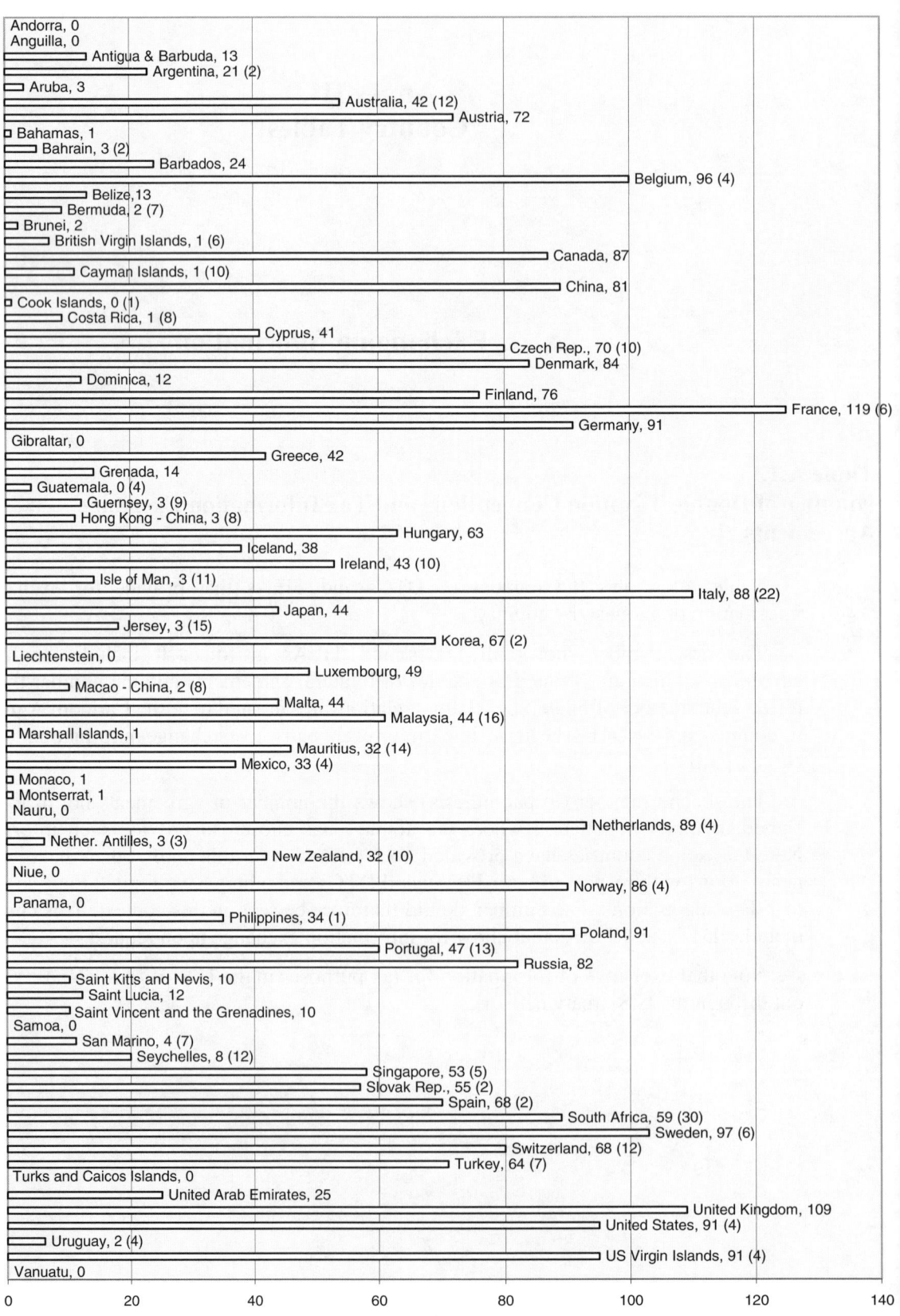

Andorra, 0
Anguilla, 0
Antigua & Barbuda, 13
Argentina, 21 (2)
Aruba, 3
Australia, 42 (12)
Austria, 72
Bahamas, 1
Bahrain, 3 (2)
Barbados, 24
Belgium, 96 (4)
Belize,13
Bermuda, 2 (7)
Brunei, 2
British Virgin Islands, 1 (6)
Canada, 87
Cayman Islands, 1 (10)
China, 81
Cook Islands, 0 (1)
Costa Rica, 1 (8)
Cyprus, 41
Czech Rep., 70 (10)
Denmark, 84
Dominica, 12
Finland, 76
France, 119 (6)
Germany, 91
Gibraltar, 0
Greece, 42
Grenada, 14
Guatemala, 0 (4)
Guernsey, 3 (9)
Hong Kong - China, 3 (8)
Hungary, 63
Iceland, 38
Ireland, 43 (10)
Isle of Man, 3 (11)
Italy, 88 (22)
Japan, 44
Jersey, 3 (15)
Korea, 67 (2)
Liechtenstein, 0
Luxembourg, 49
Macao - China, 2 (8)
Malta, 44
Malaysia, 44 (16)
Marshall Islands, 1
Mauritius, 32 (14)
Mexico, 33 (4)
Monaco, 1
Montserrat, 1
Nauru, 0
Netherlands, 89 (4)
Nether. Antilles, 3 (3)
New Zealand, 32 (10)
Niue, 0
Norway, 86 (4)
Panama, 0
Philippines, 34 (1)
Poland, 91
Portugal, 47 (13)
Russia, 82
Saint Kitts and Nevis, 10
Saint Lucia, 12
Saint Vincent and the Grenadines, 10
Samoa, 0
San Marino, 4 (7)
Seychelles, 8 (12)
Singapore, 53 (5)
Slovak Rep., 55 (2)
Spain, 68 (2)
South Africa, 59 (30)
Sweden, 97 (6)
Switzerland, 68 (12)
Turkey, 64 (7)
Turks and Caicos Islands, 0
United Arab Emirates, 25
United Kingdom, 109
United States, 91 (4)
Uruguay, 2 (4)
US Virgin Islands, 91 (4)
Vanuatu, 0

0   20   40   60   80   100   120   140

Table A.2
Summary of Domestic Laws That Permit Information Exchange in Tax Matters

This table describes the domestic laws of the countries reviewed that permit some type of information exchange in tax matters, other than laws implementing DTCs, TIEAs and MLATs.

Explanation of columns 2 and 3

Column 2 shows, in general terms, the types of domestic laws that are used by the countries reviewed to exchange information for tax purposes. Examples include mutual legal assistance laws and anti-money laundering laws that permit exchange of information for at least some tax purposes. An entry has only been made in column 2 if the relevant law allows, at a minimum, for exchange of information in tax matters with a foreign tax authority or with a foreign prosecution authority in connection with a criminal tax case. Thus, anti-money laundering legislation is referred to only where it allows for exchange of information in some tax matters and not merely because tax is a predicate offence for money laundering, under the relevant law, or because information can be exchanged between Financial Intelligence Units.

Column 3 provides commentary on the scope of the laws referred to in column 2. Where there is more than one relevant law in a particular country the commentary in column 3 is linked to the law in column 2 by one or more, asterisks "*".

Table A.2   Summary of Domestic Laws That Permit Information Exchange in Tax Matters

1	2	3
Country	**Type of Law**	**Description**
Andorra	Law implementing the Agreement between Andorra and the European Communities in relation to the EU Savings Directive.* International Judicial Co-operation.**	*Allows for exchange of information with EU Member States in matters related to tax fraud or the like in the case of savings income.[1] **International Criminal Co-operation Law allows for exchange of information in cases of tax fraud subject to the principle of dual criminality. The definition of tax fraud in Andorra is confined to fraud in relation to savings income.
Anguilla	Law implementing Savings Tax Agreements with EU Member States.	Allows for exchange of information on an automatic basis in respect of interest payments made by paying agents in Anguilla to beneficial owners who are individuals resident in EU Member States.[2]
Antigua and Barbuda	None reported.	
Argentina	None reported.	
Aruba	Law implementing Savings Tax Agreements with EU Member States.	See footnote 2.
Australia	Mutual Legal Assistance Law*	*Allows the provision, by Australia, of international assistance in criminal matters, including tax matters, when a request is made by a foreign country.
	Anti-Money Laundering Law**	**Allows for the exchange of information in criminal tax matters under the legislative powers of the Australian tax authority, e.g. where a bilateral treaty with respect to exchange of information exists.'
Austria	EU Mutual Assistance Instruments and applicable domestic law.	Allows for broad exchange of information with other EU Member States pursuant to a range of instruments.[3]
The Bahamas	None reported.	
Bahrain	Anti-Money Laundering Law.	The Bahraini Anti-Money Laundering Law permits the Bahraini competent authority to provide information to foreign authorities in criminal tax matters as defined under the laws of the foreign state seeking the information (*e.g.* where the taxpayer has committed criminal tax evasion in his country of residence and deposits the proceeds from his criminal tax evasion in a Bahraini bank).
Barbados	Mutual Legal Assistance Law.* Anti-Money Laundering Law.**	*Allows for exchange of information in criminal tax matters with Commonwealth countries and countries where a bilateral treaty with respect to mutual criminal assistance exists. **Allows for exchange of information in criminal tax matters with all countries.
Belgium	International Conventions / International judicial co-operation.* EU Mutual Assistance Instruments** and applicable domestic law.	*Allows the provision of assistance to judicial authorities in other countries in cases of serious transnational crimes including criminal tax matters punishable by more than 4 years imprisonment. **See footnote 3.

Table A.2 Summary of Domestic Laws That Permit Information Exchange in Tax Matters

1	2	3
Country	Type of Law	Description
Belize	Anti – Money Laundering Law.	Allows for exchange of information in criminal tax matters with all countries.
Bermuda	Mutual Legal Assistance Law.	Allows for exchange of information in criminal tax matters. A dual criminality requirement applies but the definition of tax fraud in Bermuda meets the OECD standard.
British Virgin Islands	Law implementing Savings Tax Agreements with EU Member States.	*Savings tax agreements provide only for exchange in the case of voluntary disclosure - See footnote 2.
Brunei	None reported.	
Canada	Mutual Legal Assistance Law.	Provides mechanisms for exchanging information in relation to criminal offences including criminal tax matters. Dual criminality is not required.
Cayman Islands	Law implementing Savings Tax Agreements with EU Member States. "The Reporting of Savings Income Information (European Union) Law 2005".	Allows for automatic exchange in respect of savings income paid to individuals - See footnote 2.
China	None reported.	
Cook Islands	Mutual Legal Assistance Law.	Allows for provision of assistance by letters of request in criminal tax matters for offences, which had they occurred in the Cook Islands, would have constituted an offence for which the maximum penalty is imprisonment for a term of not less than 12 months, or a fine of more than $5000.
Costa Rica	Anti-Money Laundering Law.	Unclear if this allows for exchange of information in criminal tax matters.
Cyprus	EU Mutual Assistance Instruments and applicable domestic law.	See footnote 3.
Czech Republic	EU Mutual Assistance Instruments and applicable domestic law.	See footnote 3.
Denmark	EU Mutual Assistance Instruments and applicable domestic law.	See footnote 3.
Dominica	None reported.	
Finland	EU Mutual Assistance Instruments and applicable domestic law.	See footnote 3.
France	EU Mutual Assistance Instruments and applicable domestic law.	See footnote 3.
Germany	Tax Law* EU Mutual Assistance Instruments** and applicable domestic law.	*German tax law permits exchange of information for tax purposes even in the absence of international agreements, provided a number of conditions are met (*i.e.* reciprocity, confidentiality, commitment to avoid double taxation, protection of trade and other secrets, no issues of ordre public/public policy). **See footnote 3.
Gibraltar	EU Mutual Assistance Instruments and applicable domestic law.	See footnote 3.

Table A.2   Summary of Domestic Laws That Permit Information Exchange in Tax Matters

1	2	3
Country	**Type of Law**	**Description**
Greece	EU Mutual Assistance Instruments and applicable domestic law.	See footnote 3.
Grenada	Anti-Money Laundering Law.	Extent to which this allows for exchange of information in criminal tax matters is unclear.
Guatemala	None reported.	
Guernsey	Fraud Investigation Law.* Mutual Legal Assistance Law.** Anti-Money Laundering Law.*** Law implementing Savings Tax Agreements with EU Member States.****	*Allows for assistance including exchange of information in cases of serious or complex fraud including tax fraud. **Allows for assistance including exchange of information in criminal tax matters which do not involve serious or complex fraud or money laundering. ***All crimes money laundering legislation which allows Guernsey's authorities to assist overseas authorities investigating criminal conduct or the whereabouts of proceeds of such conduct including tax fraud. ****Savings tax agreements provide only for exchange in the case of voluntary disclosure - See footnote 2.
Hong Kong, China	None reported.	
Hungary	EU Mutual Assistance Instruments and applicable domestic law.	See footnote 3.
Iceland	Anti-Money Laundering Law.	Extent to which this allows for exchange of information in criminal tax is unclear.
Ireland	EU Mutual Assistance Instruments and applicable domestic law.* Anti-Money Laundering Law.**	*See footnote 3. **Allows for provision of assistance to authorities in other countries investigating or prosecuting criminal offences. Fiscal offences are expressly included within the scope of the legislation.

Table A.2 Summary of Domestic Laws That Permit Information Exchange in Tax Matters

1	2	3
Country	Type of Law	Description
Isle of Man	Anti-Money Laundering Law.* Law implementing Savings Tax Agreements with EU Member States.** Criminal Justice Acts.*** Evidence (Proceedings in Other Jurisdictions) Act.****	*Allows information to be disclosed for the purposes of the prevention or detection of crime including tax crimes or for the purposes of criminal proceedings in another country. **Savings tax agreements provide only for exchange in the case of voluntary disclosure - See footnote 2. ***Allows the Attorney General to obtain and provide information relating to a suspected offence involving serious or complex fraud. The Attorney General may also obtain information for the purposes of criminal proceedings that have been instituted or a criminal investigation that is being carried on in another country. Where a request for information relates to a tax offence in respect of which proceedings have not yet been instituted, there is a requirement that the request must be from a member of the Commonwealth or is made pursuant to a treaty to which the United Kingdom is a party and which extends to the Island; if these conditions are not complied with then there is a dual criminality requirement. ****Gives effect to the Hague Convention on the Taking of Evidence Abroad in Civil and Commercial Matters.
Italy	EU Mutual Assistance Instruments and applicable domestic law.	See footnote 3.
Japan	None reported.	
Jersey	Fraud Investigation Law.* Mutual Legal Assistance Law.** Anti-Money Laundering.*** Law implementing Savings Tax Agreements with EU Member States.****	*Allows for assistance including exchange of information in cases of serious or complex fraud including tax fraud. **Allows for assistance including exchange of information in criminal matters, including tax matters. ***Allows for international co-operation with respect to money laundering which includes the laundering of the proceeds of tax crimes. ****Savings tax agreements provide only for exchange in the case of voluntary disclosure - See footnote 2.
Korea	None reported.	
Liechtenstein	Law implementing the Agreement between Liechtenstein and the European Communities in relation to the EU Savings Directive.	See footnote 1.
Luxembourg	EU Mutual Assistance Instruments and applicable domestic law.*	See footnote 3.
Macao, China	None reported.	
Malaysia	None reported.	
Malta	EU Mutual Assistance Instruments and applicable domestic law.	See footnote 3.

Table A.2   Summary of Domestic Laws That Permit Information Exchange in Tax Matters

1	2	3
Country	**Type of Law**	**Description**
Marshall Islands	Mutual Legal Assistance Law.* Anti-Money Laundering Law.**	*Allows for assistance including exchange of information in criminal tax matters, on a discretionary basis. In addition, assistance may be given where tax offence is connected to another serious offence. **Allows for assistance including exchange of information in the case of tax offences tied to other serious predicate offences but not for pure tax offences.
Mauritius	Mutual Legal Assistance Law.	*Allows for provision of assistance including obtaining information in the case of serious offences (punishable by imprisonment of 12 months or more). Serious tax offences are included.
Mexico	None reported.	
Monaco	Law implementing the Agreement between Monaco and the European Communities in relation to the EU Savings Directive.* International Judicial Co-Operation.** Law implementing assistance with respect to VAT.***	*See footnote 1. **Allows for provision of assistance by letters of request in criminal matters, including tax matters, subject to dual criminality standard. ***Applicable to all EU Member States.
Montserrat	Law implementing Savings Tax Agreements with EU Member States.	Allows for automatic exchange in respect of savings income paid to individuals - See footnote 2.
Nauru	None reported.	
Netherlands	EU Mutual Assistance Instruments and applicable domestic law.* Mutual Legal Assistance Law** Anti Money Laundering Law***	*See footnote 3. **Including assistance in fiscal offences ***Including assistance in fiscal offences
Netherlands Antilles	Law implementing Savings Tax Agreements with EU Member States.	Savings tax agreements provide only for exchange in the case of voluntary disclosure - See footnote 2.
New Zealand	Mutual Legal Assistance Law.	Allows for provision of assistance in criminal matters, including tax matters. Assistance is discretionary with any country with which New Zealand does not have an MLAT, is not on a list of prescribed countries or which is not party to a relevant multinational convention.
Niue	Mutual Legal Assistance Law.	Allows for provision of assistance in criminal matters, including tax matters, on a discretionary basis. The principle of dual criminality does not apply.
Norway	None reported.	
Panama	None reported.	
Philippines	None reported.	
Poland	EU Mutual Assistance Instruments* and applicable domestic law. Anti-Money Laundering Law.**	*See footnote 3. **Extent to which this allows for exchange of information in criminal tax matters is unclear.

Table A.2   Summary of Domestic Laws That Permit Information Exchange in Tax Matters

1	2	3
Country	Type of Law	Description
Portugal	EU Mutual Assistance Instruments and applicable domestic law.	See footnote 3.
Russian Federation	None reported.	
Saint Kitts and Nevis	Anti-Money Laundering Law.	Allows for exchange of information in cases of tax evasion where this is triable on indictment, or is a hybrid offence, in the requesting jurisdiction.
Saint Lucia	Mutual Legal Assistance Law.	Allows information to be obtained for Commonwealth countries in criminal tax matters. A dual criminality standard applies.
Saint Vincent and the Grenadines	Mutual Legal Assistance Law.	Allows for assistance to be given to Commonwealth countries in criminal matters in relation to serious or indictable offences, including tax offences. There is also provision for cooperation with non-Commonwealth countries but this is subject to amendments to the regulations.
Samoa	International Judicial Co-operation.	In connection with conduct related to fraud, misappropriation, concealment of proceeds of crime and tax evasion where some part of the offence was facilitated by a person or action in Samoa. Further, legislation on Mutual Legal Assistance in Criminal Matters, Money Laundering Prevention and Proceeds of Crime which will allow Samoa to obtain information for exchange of information purposes has been tabled in Parliament and should come into force this year.
San Marino	Anti-Money Laundering Law. * Law implementing the Agreement between San Marino and the European Communities in relation to the EU Savings Directive.** International Judicial Co-operation.***	*All-crimes money laundering legislation which, subject to the principle of dual criminality, allows tax information to be exchanged where the predicate offence of money laundering is tax-related (*e.g.* tax fraud). **See footnote 2. ***In the absence of a DTC information can be provided in criminal tax matters on the basis of letters of request, subject to a dual criminality requirement.
Seychelles	Mutual Legal Assistance Law.* Anti-Money Laundering Law.**	*Allows for exchange of information in criminal matters, which includes criminal matters relating to revenue (including taxation, customs duties or trade tax). The Act implements the Commonwealth scheme relating to mutual assistance in criminal matters within the Commonwealth and to other countries, where there is a bilateral mutual assistance treaty or to give effect to another treaty or as specified by regulation. **New anti-money laundering legislation which will continue the all crimes provisions of existing legislation is under preparation. Predicate offences will include offences under tax laws which will be open to exchange of information under the Mutual Legal Assistance Law.
Singapore	None reported.	

Table A.2 Summary of Domestic Laws That Permit Information Exchange in Tax Matters

1	2	3
Country	Type of Law	Description
Slovak Republic	EU Mutual Assistance Instruments and applicable domestic law.	See footnote 3.
South Africa	None reported.	
Spain	Mutual Legal Assistance Law.* EU Mutual Assistance Instruments** and applicable domestic law. Anti-Money Laundering Law. ***	*Allows for cooperation between judicial authorities, including cooperation in tax matters, on the basis of reciprocity. **See footnote 3. ***Extent to which this permits exchange of information for tax purposes is unclear.
Sweden	EU Mutual Assistance Instruments and applicable domestic law.	See footnote 3.
Switzerland	Mutual Legal Assistance Law.* Law implementing the Agreement between Switzerland and the European Communities in relation to the EU Savings Directive.**	*Pursuant to the Swiss federal law on mutual assistance, judicial assistance may be granted in fiscal matters if the person concerned by the foreign procedure is suspected of conduct constituting tax fraud according to Swiss law. Assistance is granted under the condition of reciprocity and is available even in the absence of an international agreement with the requesting country. Judicial assistance includes the seizure of documents and the transmission of bank information. The information obtained can only be used for prosecution of the offence and not any other purpose (*e.g.* assessment of tax). **See footnote 1.
Turkey	None reported.	
Turks and Caicos Islands	Law implementing Savings Tax Agreements with EU Member States.*	Savings tax agreements provide only for exchange in the case of voluntary disclosure - See footnote 2.
United Arab Emirates	None reported.	
United Kingdom	EU Mutual Assistance Instruments* and applicable domestic law. International Conventions / Mutual Legal Assistance Law.**	*See footnote 1. **The UK is able to provide a range of legal assistance, including to judicial and prosecuting authorities in other countries by virtue of various international conventions. It can also provide most forms of legal assistance without further bilateral or international agreements, under domestic mutual legal assistance legislation, including assistance in cases involving fiscal offences.
United States	Mutual Legal Assistance Law.	Authorizes provision of assistance to foreign and international tribunals (including criminal investigations conducted before formal accusation) in both civil and criminal tax matters.
United States Virgin Islands	Mutual Legal Assistance Law.	Authorizes provision of assistance to foreign and international tribunals (including criminal investigations conducted before formal accusation) in both civil and criminal tax matters.
Uruguay	International Judicial Co-operation.	Information in criminal tax matters may be obtained for countries with which Uruguay does not have a DTC on a court to court basis pursuant to letters of request.

Table A.2 Summary of Domestic Laws That Permit Information Exchange in Tax Matters

1	2	3
Country	**Type of Law**	**Description**
Vanuatu	Mutual Legal Assistance Law.	Allows for provision of assistance in criminal matters, including tax matters, on a discretionary basis.

[1] The European Community (EC) has entered into agreements providing for measures equivalent to those laid down in Council Directive 2003/48/EC on the taxation of savings income with Andorra, Liechtenstein, Monaco, San Marino and Switzerland. The agreements provide that the five countries concerned will withhold tax on interest payments made by paying agents established in those countries to beneficial owners who are individuals resident in EU Member States. The revenue received from the withholding tax will be shared between the withholding country and the country of the EU resident in the ratio of 25:75. The rate of withholding tax is 15% during the first three years of the agreement starting on 1 July 2005, 20% for the next three years and 35% thereafter. The agreements include a procedure which allows the beneficial owner of interest to avoid the withholding tax by authorising the paying agent to report the interest payments to the competent authority of the country in which the paying agent is established for communication to the competent authority of the country of residence of the beneficial owner. The agreements further provide for exchange of information on request on conduct constituting tax fraud or the like, under the laws of the requested state in respect of income covered by the agreement.

[2] The 27 Member States of the EU have entered into Agreements on the Taxation of Savings Income (Savings Tax Agreements) with 10 associated and dependent territories: Anguilla, Aruba, British Virgin Islands, Cayman Islands, Guernsey, Isle of Man, Jersey, Montserrat, Netherlands Antilles and the Turks and Caicos Islands. The agreements with Guernsey, Jersey, British Virgin Islands, Isle of Man, Turks and Caicos Islands and Netherlands Antilles provide for withholding tax and revenue sharing in respect of interest payments for a transitional period on the same terms as the agreements between the EC and the European third states referred to in footnote 1 above. The agreements with Anguilla, Aruba, the Cayman Islands and Montserrat provide for automatic exchange of information in respect of interest payments made by paying agents established in those countries to beneficial owners who are individuals resident in EU Member States from 1 July 2005. In general, the agreements have a two way effect and interest payments between paying agents established in EU Member States to persons resident in the associated or dependent territories are subject to automatic information exchange in most cases.

[3] Within the European Union, a number of instruments, of which the most important are the Mutual Assistance Directive 77/79/EEC (as amended), Council Regulation (EC) No 1798/2003 and Council Regulation (EC) No 2073/2004, allow for exchange of information in tax matters. The Mutual Assistance Directive provides for exchange of information in direct tax matters between all 27 EU Member States. Each of the EU Member States is required to put into force the necessary laws, regulations and administrative provisions to comply with the Directive. The Council Regulations provide for administrative co-operation between EU Member States in the field of Value Added Tax (VAT) and Excise Duties, respectively. They lay down rules and procedures to enable competent authorities of the Member States to cooperate and to exchange with each other any information that may help them effect a correct assessment of VAT and excise duties. The regulations are directly applicable in all EU Member States.

Table A.3
DTCs and TIEAs Providing for Information Exchange upon Request

Explanation of columns 2 through 5 of Table A3

Column 2 shows the number of DTCs and TIEAs, which provide for information exchange upon request, for all countries reviewed. It includes both bilateral and multilateral agreements (*e.g.* the Caricom Agreement, the Joint Council of Europe/OECD Convention on Mutual Administrative Assistance in Tax Matters, the Nordic Convention on Mutual Assistance). Multilateral agreements are counted as a series of bilateral agreements and the number therefore reflects the number of bilateral exchange relationships created (*e.g.* the Caricom Agreement is counted as 10 DTCs because it permits each party to exchange information with 10 counterparties). Further, column 2 counts every DTC and TIEA as a separate agreement even where they are entered into between the same countries. The term "TIEA" does not include limited information exchange arrangements with a very narrow scope (*e.g.* automatic exchange on certain savings related information). However, see tables A2 and A4. The numbers in column 2 match those shown in table A1, except that the number of DTCs and TIEAs in column 2 only includes TIEAs and DTCs in force (and not TIEAs or DTCs signed or under negotiation).

Column 3 shows the number of DTCs that restrict information exchange to information necessary for the application of the convention and thus do not permit information exchange for domestic tax purposes. ("limited exchange clause"). This restriction only arises in connection with DTCs.

Column 4 shows the number of DTCs and TIEAs that permit information exchange for the administration and enforcement of domestic tax laws ("broad exchange clause").

Column 5 shows for all DTCs and TIEAs included in column 4 (*i.e.* those with a broad exchange clause) whether they permit information exchange for all tax matters, only for criminal tax matters, or only for civil tax matters or certain civil tax matters.

Table A.3   DTCs and TIEAs Providing for Information Exchange upon Request

1	2		3	4	5		
Country	Type of EOI Arrangement		Limited Exchange Clause	Broad Exchange Clause	Broad Exchange Clause Covering:		
	DTC	TIEA			All Tax Matters	Only Criminal Tax Matters	Only Civil Tax Matters Or Certain Civil Tax Matters
Andorra	0	0	0	0	N/A	N/A	N/A
Anguilla	0	0	0	0	N/A	N/A	N/A
Antigua and Barbuda	12	1	1	12	12	0	0
Aruba	2	1	0	3	3	0	0
Argentina	17	4	2	19	19	0	0
Australia	42	0	1	41	41	0	0
Austria	72	0	33(25)[1]	39 (47)[2]	33[3]	0	(6)[4]
The Bahamas	0	1	0	1	1	0	0
Bahrain	3[5]	0	0	3	3	0	0
Barbados	23	1	1	23	23	0	0
Belgium	81	15	2	94	94	0	0
Belize	13	0	1	12	12	0	0
Bermuda	1	1	0	2	2	0	0
British Virgin Islands[6]	0	1	0	0	1	0	0

[1] Of the 33 DTC with limited exchange clauses, 8 are with EU members and in these cases "broad information exchange" is ensured by the application of the EU exchange mechanisms.

[2] 39 DTCs have a broad exchange clause. Broad information exchange is possible with another 8 EU countries based on EU information exchange mechanisms.

[3] In the case of 9 DTCs the transmission of information to prosecution authorities is not contemplated in the DTC but is possible based on EU information exchange mechanisms.

[4] 6 DTCs contain broad EOI clauses but they do not permit transmission of the information to prosecution authorities.

[5] Bahrain has entered into an additional 11 DTCs without specific exchange of information provisions.

[6] Note should also be taken of an agreement with Switzerland (an extension of the United Kingdom DTC with Switzerland) though not relied on in practice.

Table A.3   DTCs and TIEAs Providing for Information Exchange upon Request

1	2		3	4	5		
Country	Type of EOI Arrangement		Limited Exchange Clause	Broad Exchange Clause	Broad Exchange Clause Covering:		
	DTC	TIEA			All Tax Matters	Only Criminal Tax Matters	Only Civil Tax Matters Or Certain Civil Tax Matters
Brunei	2	0	0	2	2	0	0
Canada	86	1	1	86	86	0	0
Cayman Islands	0	1	0	0	1	0	0
China	82	0	6	76	76	0	0
Cook Islands	0	0	0	0	N/A	N/A	N/A
Costa Rica	0	1	0	1	1	0	0
Cyprus	41	0	9	32	32	0	0
Czech Republic	70	0	4	66	66	0	0
Denmark	68	16	1	83	83	0	0
Dominica	11	1	1	11	11	0	0
Finland	60	16	1	75	75	0	0
France	108	11	11	108	108	0	0
Germany	88	3	44	47	43	1	0
Gibraltar	0	0	0	0	N/A	N/A	N/A
Greece	42	0	1	41	41	0	0
Grenada	13	1	1	13	13	0	0
Guatemala	0	0	0	0	N/A	N/A	N/A
Guernsey	2	1	0	3	3	0	0
Hong Kong, China	3	0	0	3	3	0	0
Hungary	63	0	5	58	58	0	0
Iceland	22	16	1	37	37	0	0
Ireland	43	0	0	43	43	0	0

Table A.3 DTCs and TIEAs Providing for Information Exchange upon Request

1	2		3	4	5		
Country	Type of EOI Arrangement		Limited Exchange Clause	Broad Exchange Clause	Broad Exchange Clause Covering:		
	DTC	TIEA			All Tax Matters	Only Criminal Tax Matters	Only Civil Tax Matters Or Certain Civil Tax Matters
Isle of Man	1	2	0	3	3	0	0
Italy	88	0	3	85	85	0	0
Japan	44	0	3	41	41	0	0
Jersey	2	1	0	3	3	0	0
Korea	67	0	4	63	63	0	0
Liechtenstein[7]	0	0	0	0	N/A	N/A	N/A
Luxembourg	49	0	1	48	48	0	0
Macao, China	2	0	0	2	2	0	0
Malaysia	44	0	7	37	37	0	0
Malta	44	0	0	44	44	0	0
Marshall Islands	0	1	0	1	1	0	0
Mauritius	32	0	1	31	31	0	0
Mexico	31	2	1	32	32	0	0
Monaco	1	0	0	1	1	0	0
Montserrat	1	0	0	1	1	0	0
Nauru	0	0	0	0	N/A	N/A	N/A
Netherlands	78	11	23 (14)[8]	66 (75)	66 (75)	0	0
Netherlands Antilles	3	0	0	3	3	0	0
New Zealand	32	0	1	31	31	0	0

---

[7] Liechtenstein has DTCs with Austria and Switzerland but they provide for exchange of information in certain narrow circumstances only.

[8] Of the 23 DTC with limited exchange clauses, 9 are with EU members and in these cases "broad information exchange" is ensured by the application of the EU exchange mechanisms.

Table A.3   DTCs and TIEAs Providing for Information Exchange upon Request

1	2		3	4	5		
Country	Type of EOI Arrangement		Limited Exchange Clause	Broad Exchange Clause	Broad Exchange Clause Covering:		
	DTC	TIEA			All Tax Matters	Only Criminal Tax Matters	Only Civil Tax Matters Or Certain Civil Tax Matters
Niue	0	0	0	0	N/A	N/A	N/A
Norway	70	16	1	85	85	0	0
Panama	0	0	0	0	N/A	N/A	N/A
Philippines	34	0	2	32	32	0	0
Poland	81	10	0	91	91	0	0
Portugal	47	0	2	45	45	0	0
Russian Federation	65	17	1	81	81	0	0
Saint Kitts and Nevis	10	0	0	10	10	0	0
Saint Lucia	11	1	1	11	11	0	0
Saint Vincent and the Grenadines	10	0	0	10	10	0	0
Samoa	0	0	0	0	N/A	N/A	N/A
San Marino	4	0	0	4	4	0	0
Seychelles	8	0	0	8	8	0	0
Singapore	53	0	5	48	48	0	0
Slovak Republic	55	0	6	49	49	0	0
South Africa	59	0	5	54	54	0	0
Spain	68	0	1	67	67	0	0
Sweden	81	16	0	97	97	0	0
Switzerland[9][10]	68	0	64	4	0	4[11]	2

---

[9] Some Swiss conventions do not include an article dealing with exchange of information. Notwithstanding the absence of such an article exchange of information for the purposes of implementing the provisions of the convention is always possible based on a decision of the Federal Supreme Court.

Table A.3   DTCs and TIEAs Providing for Information Exchange upon Request

1	2		3	4	5		
Country	Type of EOI Arrangement		Limited Exchange Clause	Broad Exchange Clause	Broad Exchange Clause Covering:		
	DTC	TIEA			All Tax Matters	Only Criminal Tax Matters	Only Civil Tax Matters Or Certain Civil Tax Matters
Turks and Caicos Islands	0	0	0	0	N/A	N/A	N/A
Turkey	64	0	0	64	64	0	0
United Arab Emirates	25	0	10	15	15	0	0
United Kingdom	109	0	2	107	107	0	0
United States	56	35	0	91	90	1	0
United States Virgin Islands	56	35	0	91	90	1	0
Uruguay	2	0	1	1	1	0	0
Vanuatu	0	0	0	0	N/A	N/A	N/A

[10] Switzerland's DTC with Liechtenstein provides for exchange of information only in certain narrow circumstances. See footnote 7 supra.

[11] Switzerland has revised its treaties with Norway (in force), Finland (in force), Austria (signed), Spain (signed) and the United Kingdom (initialled). The revisions provide for administrative assistance relating to tax fraud or tax fraud and the like and administrative assistance for holding companies. The treaties with Norway and Finland have therefore been included under the both headings "Only Criminal Tax Matters" and "Only Civil Tax Matters or Certain Civil Tax Matters" in Column 5.

Table A4
Summary of Mechanisms That Permit Information Exchange in Tax Matters

Explanation of columns 2 through 6

Column 2 shows the number of countries with which the country identified in column 1 can exchange information in "all tax matters." "All tax matters" means that information can be exchanged for the administration and enforcement of domestic tax law in both civil and criminal tax matters.

Column 3 shows the number of countries with which the country identified in column 1 can exchange information in "certain civil tax matters." "Certain civil tax matters" means all cases where the information exchange relationship comprises less than all civil tax matters. This is the case, for instance, where information exchange is limited to information necessary for the application of the Convention (*i.e.* a limited exchange clause) or where civil exchange is limited to a particular segment of civil tax matters (*e.g.* savings information).

Column 4 shows the number of countries with which the country identified in column 1 can exchange information in criminal tax matters (or refers to agreements pursuant to which such information can be exchanged). An entry in this column means that the country is in a position to exchange information in criminal *tax* matters with a foreign tax authority or with a foreign prosecution authority in connection with a criminal tax case. The term "criminal tax matter" is used very broadly and includes any exchange for any tax matter involving conduct liable to criminal prosecution (irrespective of the particular definition used or whether exchange is subject to the principle of dual incrimination). Column 4 only shows information exchange relationships that are in addition to those already included in column 2. Thus, for example, where a country has 10 DTCs covering all tax matters (*i.e.* both civil and criminal tax matters), column 4 would show "0" provided the country has no other means to exchange information in criminal tax matters.

Column 5 includes notes that may be useful to explain entries in columns 2 through 4. The entry to which the notes relate is marked by *.

Example: Country A has 45 DTCs with a broad exchange clause and 2 DTCs with a limited exchange clause. Furthermore, under its domestic mutual assistance law, Country A can exchange information in criminal tax matters with any country that submits a valid request. Exchange of information under the mutual assistance law requires that the matter constitute a criminal tax matter as defined under the laws of Country A.

In this case column 2 would show the number 45, column 3 the number 2 and column 4 the entry "all countries." The notes column would explain that the entry in column 4 is based on the mutual assistance law of country A and "" would link the entry in columns 4 and 5.*

Table A.4   Summary of Mechanisms That Permit Information Exchange in Tax Matters

1	2	3	4	5
Country	EOI in all Tax Matters	EOI in Certain Civil Tax Matters	EOI in Criminal Tax Matters	Notes
Andorra	0	0	All countries but restrictions.*	*Information exchange is limited to cases of tax fraud related to savings income (See Table A2).
Anguilla	0	27*	1 (MLAT with the United States).	*EU Savings Tax Agreements. (See Table A2).
Antigua and Barbuda	12	1	No information.	
Aruba	3	27*	4 (MLATs).	*EU Savings Tax Agreements. (See Table A2).
Argentina	16	2		
Australia	41	1	All countries.*	See Table A2.
Austria	41*	25	3 bilateral MLATs, 39 (European Convention on Mutual Assistance in Criminal Matters, including fiscal protocol) and Schengen Agreement.	*39 DTCs have a broad exchange clause. Broad information exchange is possible with another 8 EU Member States based on EU information exchange mechanisms. Note that in relation to 6 non EU Member States information cannot be transmitted to prosecution authorities and therefore cannot be used for criminal tax matters.
The Bahamas	1*	0	0	*The Bahamas TIEA with the United States provides for exchange of information in all tax matters from the 1st of January 2006.
Bahrain	3	0	All countries.*	*The Bahraini Anti-Money Laundering Law applies to information requested in connection with criminal tax evasion as determined by reference to the laws of the requesting country. See also Table A2.
Barbados	23	1	All countries.*	*See Table A2.
Belgium	79	2	All countries.*	*See Table A2. Also note that Belgium is a party to the European Convention on Mutual Assistance in Criminal Matters, including the fiscal protocol.
Belize	12	1	1 (MLAT with United States). All countries (See Table A2).	
Bermuda	1	0	All countries (See Table A2).	
British Virgin Islands	1	0*	1 (MLAT with the United States).	*See also Table A2 for cases where voluntary disclosure can lead to exchange of information on savings income of individuals.
Brunei	2	0	No information.	
Canada	85	1	5 (MLAT).*	*MLATs (with countries without DTC or TIEA) with Antigua and Barbuda, Bahamas; Greece; Hong Kong, China; Uruguay. See Table A2.
Cayman Islands	1	27*	0	*EU Savings Tax Agreements.

Table A.4   Summary of Mechanisms That Permit Information Exchange in Tax Matters

1	2	3	4	5
Country	EOI in all Tax Matters	EOI in Certain Civil Tax Matters	EOI in Criminal Tax Matters	Notes
China	76	6	0	
Cook Islands	0	0	All countries but restrictions.*	*Allows for provision of assistance by letters of request in criminal matters, including tax matters, for which the maximum penalty is imprisonment for a term of not less than 12 months or a fine of more than $5000.
Costa Rica	1	0	Unclear whether any of the treaties or domestic laws cover tax matters.	
Cyprus	32*	9	39 (European Convention on Mutual Assistance in Criminal Matters, including fiscal protocol).	*Cyprus also exchanges information with EU Member States based on EU exchange mechanisms. See Table A2.
Czech Republic	66*	4	39 (European Convention on Mutual Assistance in Criminal Matters, including fiscal protocol) and bilateral MLATs.	*The Czech Republic also exchanges information with EU Member States based on EU exchange mechanisms. See Table A2.
Denmark	74*	1	39 (European Convention on Mutual Assistance in Criminal Matters, including fiscal protocol).	*Denmark also exchanges information with EU Member States based on EU exchange mechanisms. See Table A2.
Dominica	11	1	No information.	
Finland	67*	1	39 (European Convention on Mutual Assistance in Criminal Matters, including fiscal protocol).	*Finland also exchanges information with EU Member States based on EU exchange mechanisms. See Table A2.
France	109*	11	46 (European Convention on Mutual Assistance in Criminal Matters, including fiscal protocol); a number of bilateral MLATs; Schengen Agreement.	*France also exchanges information with EU Member States based on EU exchange mechanisms. See Table A2.
Germany	All countries*	0	39 (European Convention on Mutual Assistance in Criminal Matters, including fiscal protocol), a number of bilateral legal assistance arrangements, Schengen Agreement.	*Pursuant to domestic law and subject to certain conditions. Furthermore Germany exchanges information with EU Member States based on EU exchange mechanisms. See Table A2.
Gibraltar	27*	0	0	*Gibraltar exchanges information with EU Member States based on EU exchange mechanisms. See Table A2.
Greece	41*	1	39 (European Convention on Mutual Assistance in Criminal Matters, including fiscal protocol).	*Greece also exchanges information with EU Member States based on EU exchange mechanisms. See Table A2.
Grenada	13	1	No information.	
Guatemala	0*	0	0	*Guatemala has signed a convention on exchange of information with Central American countries, but it has not yet come into force.

Table A.4   Summary of Mechanisms That Permit Information Exchange in Tax Matters

1	2	3	4	5
Country	EOI in all Tax Matters	EOI in Certain Civil Tax Matters	EOI in Criminal Tax Matters	Notes
Guernsey	3*	0**	All countries (See Table A2).	*A TIEA between Guernsey and the US with respect to civil and criminal tax matters is now in force. **See also Table A2 for cases where voluntary disclosure can lead to exchange of information on savings income of individuals.
Hong Kong, China	3	0	0	
Hungary	63*	0	39 (European Convention on Mutual Assistance in Criminal Matters, including fiscal protocol).	*Hungary also exchanges information with EU Member States based on EU exchange mechanisms. See Table A2.
Iceland	27	1	39 (European Convention on Mutual Assistance in Criminal Matters, including fiscal protocol).	
Ireland	43*	0	All countries. (See Table A2).**	*Ireland also exchanges information with EU Member States based on EU exchange mechanisms. See Table A2. **Ireland has also ratified the European Convention on Mutual Assistance in Criminal Matters, including the fiscal protocol.
Isle of Man	3	0*	All countries. (See Table A2).	*See also Table A2 for cases where voluntary disclosure can lead to exchange of information on savings income of individuals.
Italy	85*	3	39 (European Convention on Mutual Assistance in Criminal Matters, including fiscal protocol); number of bilateral legal assistance arrangements.	*Italy also exchanges information with EU Member States based on EU exchange mechanisms and on the OECD-Council of Europe Convention on Mutual Administrative Assistance in Tax Matters. See Table A2.
Japan	41	3	0	
Jersey	3	0*	All countries. (See Table A2).	*See also Table A2 for cases where voluntary disclosure can lead to exchange of information on savings income of individuals.
Korea	63	4	0	
Liechtenstein	0	0	1 (MLAT with United States) + 27.*	*Liechtenstein exchanges information with EU Member States in cases of tax fraud related to savings income. (See Table A2).
Luxembourg	48	1	39 (European Convention on Mutual Assistance in Criminal Matters, including fiscal protocol), 1 MLAT with United States.	*Luxembourg also exchanges information with EU Member States based on EU exchange mechanisms. See Table A2.
Macao, China	2	0	Signatory to certain international conventions. (See Table A2).	
Malaysia	37	7		

Table A.4   Summary of Mechanisms That Permit Information Exchange in Tax Matters

1	2	3	4	5
Country	EOI in all Tax Matters	EOI in Certain Civil Tax Matters	EOI in Criminal Tax Matters	Notes
Malta	44	0	0	*Malta also exchanges information with EU Member States based on EU exchange mechanisms. See Table A2.
Marshall Islands	1	0	All countries but restrictions.*	*Discretionary powers under the Mutual Assistance in Criminal Matters Act (2002). See Table A2.
Mauritius	31	1	All countries. (See Table A2).	
Mexico	30	1	0	
Monaco	1	0	27* & All countries.**	*Monaco exchanges information with EU members in connection with VAT fraud and in cases of tax fraud related to savings income. See Table A2. **Monaco provides information in foreign criminal tax investigations under its rules on international rogatory letters.
Montserrat	1	27**	1 (MLAT with the United States).	**EU Savings Tax Agreement.
Nauru	0	0	0	
Netherlands	75*	14	39 (European Convention on Mutual Assistance in Criminal Matters, including fiscal protocol).	*The Netherlands also exchanges information with EU Member States based on EU exchange mechanisms. See Table A2.
Netherlands Antilles	3*	0**	0	*The Netherlands Antilles has also signed a TIEA with the United States, which came into force in March 2007. **See also Table A2 for cases where voluntary disclosure can lead to exchange of information on savings income of individuals.
New Zealand	31	1	All countries. (See Table 2).	
Niue	0	0	All countries but restrictions.*	*Discretionary powers under the Mutual Assistance in Criminal Matters Act. See Table A 2.
Norway	76	1	39 (European Convention on Mutual Assistance in Criminal Matters, including fiscal protocol); Schengen Agreement, MLAT with Thailand.	
Panama	0	0	1 (MLAT with the United States) with restrictions.*	*Tax offences are excluded from the MLAT unless it is shown that the money involved derives from an activity that itself is a covered offence (*e.g.* tax prosecution involving unreported income from drug trafficking).
Philippines	32	2	0	
Poland	81*	0	39 (European Convention on Mutual Assistance in Criminal Matters, including fiscal protocol).	Poland also exchanges information with EU Member States based on EU exchange mechanisms. See Table A2.
Portugal	45*	2	39 (European Convention on Mutual Assistance in Criminal Matters, including fiscal protocol).	Portugal also exchanges information with EU Member States based on EU exchange mechanisms. See Table A2.

Russian Federation	81	1	0	
Saint Kitts and Nevis	10	0	1 (MLAT with the United States). All countries.**	**The anti-money laundering law covers tax evasion. See Table A2.
Saint Lucia	11	1	1 (MLAT with the United States). Commonwealth countries (See Table A2).	
Saint Vincent and the Grenadines	10	0	1 (MLAT with the United States). Commonwealth countries (See Table A2).	
Samoa	0	0	All countries but restrictions. (See Table A2).	
San Marino	4*	0	2**+ 27***+ All countries.****	*DTCs with Austria, Croatia, Luxembourg and Malta are in force. **Agreements in force with Italy and France permitting exchange of information in criminal tax matters. ***For conduct constituting tax fraud or the like relating to savings income San Marino provides information to EU Member States for civil and criminal tax purposes. ****See Table A2.
Seychelles	8	0	Commonwealth countries + other identified countries in the Mutual Assistance Act. (See Table A2).	
Singapore	48	5	0	
Slovak Republic	49	6	39 (European Convention on Mutual Assistance in Criminal Matters, including fiscal protocol).	The Slovak Republic also exchanges information with EU Member States based on EU exchange mechanisms. See Table A2.
South Africa	54	5		
Spain	67*	1	All countries.**	*Spain also exchanges information with EU Member States based on EU exchange mechanisms. See Table A2. **Pursuant to Spain's Anti-Money Laundering law and judicial co-operation law. Spain has also ratified the European Convention on Mutual Assistance in Criminal Matters (including fiscal protocol).
Sweden	97	0	39 (European Convention on Mutual Assistance in Criminal Matters, including fiscal protocol).	*Sweden also exchanges information with EU Member States based on EU exchange mechanisms. See Table A2.
Switzerland	0	68	6 MLATs & all countries. (See Table A2).*	*Note that under the principle of speciality, information provided pursuant to the Swiss Mutual Assistance Law can only be used for prosecution purposes. No such restriction on the use of the information applies where the information is provided pursuant to a DTC.
Turkey	64	0	39 (European Convention on Mutual Assistance in Criminal Matters, including fiscal protocol); number of bilateral MLATs.	
Turks and Caicos Islands	0	0*	1 (MLAT with the United States).	*See also Table A2 for cases where voluntary disclosure can lead to exchange of information on savings income of individuals.

Table A.4 Summary of Mechanisms That Permit Information Exchange in Tax Matters

1	2	3	4	5
Country	EOI in all Tax Matters	EOI in Certain Civil Tax Matters	EOI in Criminal Tax Matters	Notes
United Arab Emirates	15	10	10 bilateral MLATs and 2 multilateral conventions.	.
United Kingdom	107*	2	All countries. (See Table A2).**	*The United Kingdom also exchanges information with EU Member States based on EU exchange mechanisms. See Table A2. **The United Kingdom has also ratified European Convention on Mutual Assistance in Criminal Matters (including fiscal protocol).
United States	77*	1	Organisation of American States MLAT (including optional protocol), number of bilateral MLATs.	*The United States can also provide certain information in both civil and criminal tax matters to all countries. See Table A2.
United States Virgin Islands	77*	1	Organisation of American States MLAT (including optional protocol), number of bilateral MLATs.**	*The United States can also provide certain information in both civil and criminal tax matters to all countries. See Table A2. Unclear whether this applies to the United States Virgin Islands. **Unclear whether applies to United States Virgin Islands.
Uruguay	1	1	All countries. (See Table A2).	
Vanuatu	0	0	All countries but restricted.*	*Discretionary powers under the Mutual Assistance in Criminal Matters Act (2002) but no exchange in pure tax matters has taken place.

Table A.5
Application of Dual Criminality Principle

This table shows the application of the principle of dual criminality for all countries reviewed that restrict information exchange on request for the application or enforcement of the domestic tax law of the requesting country to criminal tax matters. Note that countries that have one or more mechanisms in place that (for the purposes of the administration or enforcement of domestic law) permit information exchange in both civil and criminal tax matters do not appear in the table.

Explanation of columns 2 through 4

Column 2 shows whether the principle of dual criminality is applied to the exchange of information for criminal tax purposes. **Column 3** describes the various laws and instruments used by the countries mentioned in the table to provide information in criminal tax matters.

Column 4 provides a general understanding of the standard of criminality that applies in the countries concerned in so far as exchange of information in criminal tax matters is concerned. Where there is more than one relevant law or instrument the commentary in column 4 is linked to the law in column 3 by one or more "*".

Table A.5   Application of Dual Criminality Principle

1	2	3	4
Country	**Application of the principle of dual criminality**	**Type of law/instrument**	**Standard used to determine criminality**
Andorra	Yes	Law implementing the Agreement between Andorra and the European Communities in relation to the EU Savings Directive.* International Judicial Co-operation.**	*Tax fraud or the like. Tax fraud occurs where a person, deceitfully and in order to profit, defrauds the administration in matters of the taxation of savings income by falsifying documents or using false or incorrect titles with regard to their content. The like includes only an offence with the same level of wrongfulness as conduct constituting tax fraud under the laws of the requested state. **See above for definition of tax fraud.
Anguilla	Not for tax purposes.	MLAT with the United States.[1]	The principle of dual criminality applies. Subject to two exceptions, however, a criminal offence does not include any conduct or matter which relates directly or indirectly to the regulation, imposition, calculation or collection of taxes. The exceptions are the fraudulent promotion of tax shelters and tax offences relating to the proceeds of other criminal offences for which assistance may be granted.
Cook Islands	Yes	Mutual Assistance Act.	Criminal matters includes offences against a provision of a law of a foreign country in relation to acts or omissions which, had they occurred in the Cook Islands, would have constituted an offence for which the maximum penalty is imprisonment for a term of not less than 12 months or a fine of more than $5000.
Liechtenstein	No.* However the requested state may decline a request to the extent the conduct would not constitute an offence under its laws and the execution of the request would require a court order for search and seizure or other coercive measures. Yes.**	*MLAT with the United States. **Law implementing the Agreement between Liechtenstein and the European Communities in relation to the EU Savings Directive.	**Tax fraud or the like for income covered by the agreement. The like only includes offences with the same level of wrongfulness as conduct constituting tax fraud under the laws of the requested state.
Montserrat	Not for tax purposes.	MLAT with the United States.	See commentary on Anguilla. The same treaty applies to Montserrat.
Niue	No	Mutual Legal Assistance Law.	The Attorney General may authorise the taking of evidence or the production of documents in Niue to assist other countries in proceedings or investigations of criminal matters. Criminal matters include criminal matters relating to revenue including taxation and custom offences whether arising under Niue law or the law of a foreign country.

---

[1] The treaty between the United Kingdom and the United States concerning the Cayman Islands relating to Mutual Legal Assistance in Criminal Matters has been extended to Anguilla, the British Virgin Islands, Montserrat and the Turks and Caicos Islands.

Table A.5   Application of Dual Criminality Principle

1	2	3	4
Country	**Application of the principle of dual criminality**	**Type of law/instrument**	**Standard used to determine criminality**
Panama	Not for tax purposes.	MLAT with the United States.	The principle of dual criminality applies subject to exceptions. However, tax matters are excluded from the definition of offence under the treaty unless it is shown that the money involved derived from an activity that otherwise falls under the definition of an offence. For example, assistance could be given in the case of a criminal prosecution involving unreported income derived from drug trafficking because drug trafficking is a prescribed offence.
Samoa	Yes	International Judicial Co-operation.	Conduct related to fraud, misappropriation, concealment of proceeds of crime and tax evasion where some part of the offence was facilitated by a person or action in Samoa.
Turks and Caicos Islands	Not for tax purposes.	MLAT.	See commentary on Anguilla. The same treaty applies to the Turks and Caicos Islands.
Vanuatu	No. However a potential ground for refusing a request for assistance is that the request relates to the prosecution or punishment of a person for an act that had it occurred in Vanuatu would not have constituted an offence under Vanuatu law.	Mutual Legal Assistance Law.	The Attorney General may authorise the taking of evidence or the production of documents in Vanuatu to assist other countries in proceedings or investigations of criminal tax matters in those countries. To date this power has not been used in a pure tax matter that is tax matters that are not tainted by some other element of illegality.

B.   Access to Bank Information

Table B.1
Bank Secrecy

Explanation of columns 2 through 4

Table B 1 shows for all of the countries reviewed whether the basis for bank secrecy arises purely out of the relationship between the bank and its customer (e.g. contract, privacy, common law) (**column 2**), whether it is reinforced by statute (**column 3**) and, if reinforced by statute, whether the statutory provisions are limited to particular customers or market segments (**column 4**). Note that in some countries there are separate laws providing for secrecy in domestic and international banking business. The entry in column 4 in these cases is "No" provided the level of banking confidentiality is similar.

Table B.1   Bank Secrecy

1	2	3	4
Country	Bank secrecy based purely on contract/privacy/common law	Bank secrecy reinforced by statute	Statutory bank secrecy rules limited to particular customers or market segments
Andorra	No	Yes	No
Anguilla	No	Yes	No
Antigua and Barbuda	Yes	No	N/A
Aruba	No	Yes	No
Argentina	No	Yes	No
Australia	Yes	No	N/A
Austria	No	Yes	No
The Bahamas	No	Yes	No
Bahrain	No	Yes	No
Barbados	No	Yes	No
Belgium	Yes	No	N/A
Belize	No	Yes	No
Bermuda	Yes	No	N/A
British Virgin Islands	Yes	No	N/A
Brunei	No	Yes	More information required
Canada	Yes	No	N/A
Cayman Islands	No	Yes	No
China	No	Yes	No
Cook Islands	No	Yes	No
Costa Rica	No	Yes	No
Cyprus	No	Yes	No
Czech Republic	No	Yes	No
Denmark	No	Yes	No
Dominica	No	Yes	Offshore banks
Finland	No	Yes	No
France	No	Yes	No
Germany	Yes	No	N/A
Gibraltar	Yes	No	N/A
Greece	No	Yes	No
Grenada	No	Yes	International banks

Table B.1   Bank Secrecy

1	2	3	4
Country	Bank secrecy based purely on contract/privacy/common law	Bank secrecy reinforced by statute	Statutory bank secrecy rules limited to particular customers or market segments
Guatemala	No	Yes	No
Guernsey	Yes	No	N/A
Hong Kong, China	Yes	No	N/A
Hungary	Yes	No	N/A
Iceland	No	Yes	No
Ireland	Yes	No	N/A
Isle of Man	Yes	No	N/A
Italy	Yes	No	N/A
Japan	Yes	No	N/A
Jersey	Yes	No	N/A
Korea	No	Yes	No
Liechtenstein	No	Yes	No
Luxembourg	No	Yes	No
Macao, China	No	Yes	No
Malaysia	No	Yes	Yes (Labuan)
Malta	No	Yes	No
Marshall Islands	No	Yes	No
Montserrat	No	Yes	No
Mauritius	No	Yes	No
Mexico	No	Yes	No
Monaco	No	Yes	No
Nauru	No	Yes	No
Netherlands	Yes	No	N/A
Netherlands Antilles	Yes	No	N/A
New Zealand	Yes	No	N/A
Niue	No	Yes	No
Norway	No	Yes	No
Panama	No	Yes	No
Philippines	No	Yes	No
Poland	No	Yes	No

Table B.1   Bank Secrecy

1	2	3	4
Country	Bank secrecy based purely on contract/privacy/common law	Bank secrecy reinforced by statute	Statutory bank secrecy rules limited to particular customers or market segments
Portugal	No	Yes	No
Russian Federation	No	Yes	No
Saint Kitts and Nevis	No	Yes	No
Saint Lucia	No	Yes	No
Saint Vincent and the Grenadines	No	Yes	No
Samoa	No	Yes	International banks
San Marino	No	Yes	No
Seychelles	No	Yes	No
Singapore	No	Yes	No
Slovak Republic	No	Yes	No
South Africa	Yes	No	N/A
Spain	No	Yes	No
Sweden	No	Yes	No
Switzerland	No	Yes	No
Turkey	No	Yes	No
Turks and Caicos Islands	No	Yes	No
United Arab Emirates	Yes	No	No
United Kingdom	Yes	No	N/A
United States	No	Yes	No
United States Virgin Islands	No	Yes	No
Uruguay	No	Yes	No
Vanuatu	No	Yes	International banking

Table B.2
Access to Bank Information for Exchange of Information Purposes

Explanation of columns 2 through 7

Table B2 shows to what extent the countries reviewed have access to bank information for exchange of information purposes in all tax matters (**column 2**), which countries have access in all tax matters only if information is also relevant for domestic tax purposes (domestic tax interest) (**column 3**), which countries can have access to bank information only in criminal tax matters and the standard these countries use to determine what is a "criminal tax matter" (**columns 4 and 5**) and which countries have no access to bank information for any tax information exchange purposes (**column 6**). Some additional and explanatory comments are provided in **column 7**.

Table B.2   Access to Bank Information for Exchange of Information Purposes

1	2	3	4	5	6	7
Country	Ability to obtain bank info for EOI purposes in all tax matters	Ability to obtain bank info for EOI purposes in all tax matters only if domestic tax interest present	Ability to obtain bank info for EOI purposes only in criminal tax matters	If ability restricted to criminal tax matters, standard used to determine "criminal tax matters"	Inability to obtain bank information for any tax information exchange purposes	Notes/Other
Andorra	No	No	Yes*	See Table A5.	No	*Information can be obtained in relation to savings income in cases of tax fraud or the like pursuant to the Savings Agreement with the European Communities and in cases of tax fraud pursuant to the International Criminal Co-operation Law. (See Table A2).
Anguilla	No*	No	Yes**	See Table A5.	No	*Anguilla exchanges information automatically on savings income under its bilateral agreements with EU Member States. **With respect to the MLAT with the United States.
Antigua and Barbuda	Yes*	No	N/A	N/A	No	*Under its TIEA with the United States.
Argentina	Yes	No	N/A	N/A	No	
Aruba	Yes	No	N/A	N/A	No	
Australia	Yes	No	N/A	N/A	No	

Table B.2 Access to Bank Information for Exchange of Information Purposes

1	2	3	4	5	6	7
Country	Ability to obtain bank info for EOI purposes in all tax matters	Ability to obtain bank info for EOI purposes in all tax matters only if domestic tax interest present	Ability to obtain bank info for EOI purposes only in criminal tax matters	If ability restricted to criminal tax matters, standard used to determine "criminal tax matters"	Inability to obtain bank information for any tax information exchange purposes	Notes/Other
Austria	No	No	Yes*	"Intentional fiscal offences" with the exception of fiscal misdemeanours. Intentional fiscal violations are understood to be cases of tax evasion defined as "someone is guilty of tax evasion if he or she intentionally effectuates a loss of revenue through non-compliance with fiscal requirements for reporting, disclosure of facts or truth obligations." Falsifications of documents or other fraudulent actions are not required.	No	*Note that as a procedural matter criminal proceeding must have been commenced (either within the tax administration or by a court). Due to a recent Supreme Administrative Court ruling the taxpayer has to be notified on that proceeding through a formal notice which is subject to the opportunity of appeal proceedings.
The Bahamas	Yes*	No*	N/A*	N/A*	N/A	*Pursuant to its TIEA with the United States The Bahamas has the ability to obtain bank information in all tax matters for taxable periods commencing on or after January 1, 2006, and there is no requirement for the presence of a domestic tax interest as a pre-condition to dealing with a request.
Bahrain	Yes*	No	N/A	N/A	No	*Outside the context of a DTC with standard exchange of information clauses, Bahrain may also obtain information from banks and other financial institutions (i) through a court order, (ii) pursuant to its anti-money laundering law in criminal tax matters, or (iii) with the unequivocal approval of the person to whom the confidential information relates.

Table B.2 Access to Bank Information for Exchange of Information Purposes

1 Country	2 Ability to obtain bank info for EOI purposes in all tax matters	3 Ability to obtain bank info for EOI purposes in all tax matters only if domestic tax interest present	4 Ability to obtain bank info for EOI purposes only in criminal tax matters	5 If ability restricted to criminal tax matters, standard used to determine "criminal tax matters"	6 Inability to obtain bank information for any tax information exchange purposes	7 Notes/Other
Barbados	Yes*	No	N/A	N/A	No	*In Barbados some laws restrict information only to the domestic tax authorities. Barbados does not exchange information on low tax entities that are excluded from the scope of its tax treaties. These laws, however, can be overridden by a DTC and TIEA.
Belgium	No*	No	No*	Bank secrecy can be lifted if the Belgian bank has conducted "abnormal banking operations" (in particular tax fraud supporting acts) or if a tax audit reveals concrete elements of the existence or the preparation of a mechanism of tax fraud.	No	*Only in the case of an administrative appeal the tax authorities have access to bank information if the taxpayer refuses to provide it. In all other cases, access to bank information is restricted to criminal tax matters (see column 5). Note however that Belgium will exchange bank information on request for civil (and criminal) tax matters within the framework of the new DTC with the United States (signed on 27 November 2006)
Belize	No	No	Yes	Criminal offence in requesting country.	No	
Bermuda	Yes*	No	N/A	N/A	No	*Under a DTC and TIEA entered into with another country. In relation to other countries Bermuda can obtain bank information for tax information exchange purposes in criminal tax matters.

Table B.2 Access to Bank Information for Exchange of Information Purposes

1	2	3	4	5	6	7
Country	Ability to obtain bank info for EOI purposes in all tax matters	Ability to obtain bank info for EOI purposes in all tax matters only if domestic tax interest present	Ability to obtain bank info for EOI purposes only in criminal tax matters	If ability restricted to criminal tax matters, standard used to determine "criminal tax matters"	Inability to obtain bank information for any tax information exchange purposes	Notes/Other
British Virgin Islands	Yes*	No	N/A	N/A	No	The British Virgin Islands has the power to obtain bank information pursuant to the Mutual Legal Assistance (Tax Matters) Act 2003 The British Virgin Islands - United States TIEA provides for exchange of information in all tax matters.
Brunei	No information	No information	No information	No information	No information	
Canada	Yes	No	N/A	N/A	No	
Cayman Islands	Yes*	No	N/A	N/A	No	*The Cayman Islands has the power to obtain bank information in all tax matters for the purposes of its tax information agreements. The Cayman Islands also exchanges information automatically on savings income under its bilateral agreements with EU Member States.
China	Yes	No	N/A	N/A	No	The tax authorities have access to bank information for the purposes of responding to a request for exchange of information with treaty partners provided the relevant DTC or TIEA so allows. The tax authorities may enquire into the deposit accounts that a taxpayer engaged in production or business or a withholding agent has opened with banks or other financial institutions. Further, in investigating a case involving a violation of tax laws the tax authorities may investigate the savings deposits of an individual.

Table B.2 Access to Bank Information for Exchange of Information Purposes

1	2	3	4	5	6	7
Country	Ability to obtain bank info for EOI purposes in all tax matters	Ability to obtain bank info for EOI purposes in all tax matters only if domestic tax interest present	Ability to obtain bank info for EOI purposes only in criminal tax matters	If ability restricted to criminal tax matters, standard used to determine "criminal tax matters"	Inability to obtain bank information for any tax information exchange purposes	Notes/Other
Cook Islands	No	No	Yes*	See Table A5.	No	*Subject to conditions that the Attorney General determines.
Costa Rica	Yes*	No	N/A	N/A	No	*Under the TIEA with the United States, Costa Rica is required to provide information relating to banks with the authorisation of the Judge of Administrative Trials, who will grant it, unless good cause is shown that the information is not related to the enforcement of laws relating to a possible tax fraud matter. Tax fraud is very broadly defined in Costa Rica.
Cyprus	No*	Yes	N/A	N/A	No	Cyprus exchanges bank information relating to savings income with other EU Member States pursuant to legislation implementing the EU Savings Directive. Otherwise a domestic tax interest is required to obtain access to bank information.
Czech Republic	Yes	No	N/A	N/A	No	
Denmark	Yes	No	N/A	N/A	No	
Dominica	No information	No information	No information	No information	No information	
Finland	Yes	No	N/A	N/A	No	
France	Yes	No	N/A	N/A	No	
Germany	Yes	No	N/A	N/A	No	

Table B.2   Access to Bank Information for Exchange of Information Purposes

1	2	3	4	5	6	7
Country	Ability to obtain bank info for EOI purposes in all tax matters	Ability to obtain bank info for EOI purposes in all tax matters only if domestic tax interest present	Ability to obtain bank info for EOI purposes only in criminal tax matters	If ability restricted to criminal tax matters, standard used to determine "criminal tax matters"	Inability to obtain bank information for any tax information exchange purposes	Notes/Other
Gibraltar	No*	No*	No	N/A	No*	*Gibraltar has enacted legislation to permit the automatic exchange of information with the EU Member States in accordance with the Savings Directive.
Greece	Yes	No	N/A	N/A	No	
Grenada	Yes*	No	N/A	N/A	No	*Under TIEA with United States.
Guatemala	No	No	No	N/A	Yes	
Guernsey	Yes*	No	N/A	N/A.	No	*In its TIEA with the United States Guernsey has agreed to exchange of information, including bank information, in civil tax matters. Guernsey has enacted legislation to allow it to obtain bank information for the purposes of the TIEA. In relation to other countries Guernsey can obtain bank information for tax information exchange purposes in criminal tax matters.
Hong Kong, China	No	Yes	N/A	N/A	No	
Hungary	Yes	No	N/A	N/A	No	
Iceland	Yes	No	N/A	N/A	No	
Ireland	Yes	No	N/A	N/A	No	

Table B.2 Access to Bank Information for Exchange of Information Purposes

1	2	3	4	5	6	7
Country	**Ability to obtain bank info for EOI purposes in all tax matters**	**Ability to obtain bank info for EOI purposes in all tax matters only if domestic tax interest present**	**Ability to obtain bank info for EOI purposes only in criminal tax matters**	**If ability restricted to criminal tax matters, standard used to determine "criminal tax matters"**	**Inability to obtain bank information for any tax information exchange purposes**	**Notes/Other**
Isle of Man	Yes*	No	N/A	N/A	No	* An Isle of Man DTC or TIEA has as standard text the ability to obtain bank information in response to a request for both civil and criminal tax purposes. In relation to other countries the Isle of Man can obtain bank information for tax information exchange purposes in criminal tax matters.
Italy	Yes	No	N/A	N/A	No	
Japan	Yes	No	N/A	N/A	No	
Jersey	Yes*	No	N/A	N/A	No	* Jersey has enacted legislation which enables it to obtain bank and other information for the purposes of the TIEA with the US. Equivalent legislative provisions will be enacted for the purposes of other TIEAs as and when they are concluded. Notwithstanding the absence of a TIEA or DTC, for all countries, Jersey can obtain bank and other information for tax information exchange purposes in criminal tax matters.
Korea	Yes	No	N/A	N/A	No	

Table B.2 Access to Bank Information for Exchange of Information Purposes

1	2	3	4	5	6	7
Country	Ability to obtain bank info for EOI purposes in all tax matters	Ability to obtain bank info for EOI purposes in all tax matters only if domestic tax interest present	Ability to obtain bank info for EOI purposes only in criminal tax matters	If ability restricted to criminal tax matters, standard used to determine "criminal tax matters"	Inability to obtain bank information for any tax information exchange purposes	Notes/Other
Liechtenstein	No	No	Yes*	Under the MLAT: Tax matters "where the conduct described constitutes tax fraud, defined as tax evasion committed by means of the intentional use of false, falsified or incorrect business records or other documents, provided the tax due, either as an absolute amount or in relation to an annual amount due, is substantial." Under the Savings Agreement with the EC: Conduct constituting tax fraud under the laws of the requested State, or the like for income covered by this Agreement. "The like" includes only offences with the same level of wrongfulness as is the case for tax fraud under the laws of the requested State.	No	*Under the MLAT with the United States. Under the Savings Agreement with the EC, information can be provided in matters related to tax fraud or "the like" in the case of savings income. (See Table A2).
Luxembourg	No	No	Yes	Tax fraud (escroquerie fiscale) exists if a significant amount is involved, either in absolute terms or by reference to the yearly tax due, and it has been realized by a systematic use of fraudulent stratagems aimed at concealing facts relevant to the authority or at persuading the authority of inaccurate facts.	No	

Table B.2   Access to Bank Information for Exchange of Information Purposes

1	2	3	4	5	6	7
Country	Ability to obtain bank info for EOI purposes in all tax matters	Ability to obtain bank info for EOI purposes in all tax matters only if domestic tax interest present	Ability to obtain bank info for EOI purposes only in criminal tax matters	If ability restricted to criminal tax matters, standard used to determine "criminal tax matters"	Inability to obtain bank information for any tax information exchange purposes	Notes/Other
Macao, China	No	No	Yes	The Penal Code contains the list of conducts that in general qualify as a crime. There are no special legal provisions for tax crimes. A criminal tax matter is a concept that falls in the said general provisions such as fraud, forgery, fraud in bankruptcy, etc.	No	
Malaysia	No*	No*	Response is unclear.**	No information	No	*The Tax Authorities have indirect access to bank information (through the account holder) where there is a domestic tax interest. **Unclear if information can be obtained in criminal tax matters in relation to Labuan.
Malta	No*	No	Yes	Based on 2003 OECD common understanding of tax fraud.	No	*Malta exchanges bank information relating to savings income with other EU Member States pursuant to legislation implementing the EU Savings Directive.
Marshall Islands	Yes*	No	N/A	N/A	No	*With respect to the TIEA with the United States. In other cases, only in criminal tax matters on a discretionary basis (See Table A2).
Mauritius	Yes	No	N/A	N/A	No	
Mexico	Yes	No	N/A	N/A	No	

Table B.2   Access to Bank Information for Exchange of Information Purposes

1	2	3	4	5	6	7
Country	Ability to obtain bank info for EOI purposes in all tax matters	Ability to obtain bank info for EOI purposes in all tax matters only if domestic tax interest present	Ability to obtain bank info for EOI purposes only in criminal tax matters	If ability restricted to criminal tax matters, standard used to determine "criminal tax matters"	Inability to obtain bank information for any tax information exchange purposes	Notes/Other
Monaco	Yes*	No	N/A	N/A	No	*With respect to France. In other cases, Monaco only exchanges information in criminal tax matters subject to a dual criminality standard. Under the Savings Agreement with the EU, information can be provided in matters related to tax fraud in the case of savings income. (See Table A2).
Montserrat	No*	No	Yes**	See Table A5.	No	*Montserrat provides information automatically on savings income under the bilateral agreements with the EU Member States. **Montserrat can exchange information in criminal tax matters under the MLAT with the United States.
Nauru	No	No	No	N/A	Yes	Nauru's laws do not provide access to bank information for tax purposes.
Netherlands	Yes	No	N/A	N/A	No	
Netherlands Antilles	Yes	No	N/A	N/A	No	
New Zealand	Yes	No	N/A	N/A	No	
Niue	No	No	Yes*	Criminal tax matters arise under Niue laws or those of a foreign country.	No	*On a discretionary basis. (See Table A2).
Norway	Yes	No	N/A	N/A	No	N/A

Table B.2 Access to Bank Information for Exchange of Information Purposes

1	2	3	4	5	6	7
Country	Ability to obtain bank info for EOI purposes in all tax matters	Ability to obtain bank info for EOI purposes in all tax matters only if domestic tax interest present	Ability to obtain bank info for EOI purposes only in criminal tax matters	If ability restricted to criminal tax matters, standard used to determine "criminal tax matters"	Inability to obtain bank information for any tax information exchange purposes	Notes/Other
Panama	No	No	No*	N/A	No*	*The MLAT with the United States allows for information exchange in connection with certain criminal tax matters related to other covered non tax offences (See Table A5). It is unclear if this would allow access to bank information.
Philippines	No	No*	No	N/A	Yes*	*The ability of the Commissioner of the Internal Revenue to obtain bank information is restricted to two cases: for a decedent to determine the estate and for a taxpayer to prove the incapacity to pay. These restrictions are not applied in relation to financial institutions, other than banks, provided there is a domestic tax interest.
Poland	Yes	No	N/A	N/A	No	

Table B.2   Access to Bank Information for Exchange of Information Purposes

1	2	3	4	5	6	7
Country	Ability to obtain bank info for EOI purposes in all tax matters	Ability to obtain bank info for EOI purposes in all tax matters only if domestic tax interest present	Ability to obtain bank info for EOI purposes only in criminal tax matters	If ability restricted to criminal tax matters, standard used to determine "criminal tax matters"	Inability to obtain bank information for any tax information exchange purposes	Notes/Other
Portugal	Yes*	No*	N/A	N/A	No	*Access to bank information is possible where there are indications of a tax crime or concrete identified facts that a taxpayer provided false information to the tax administration. The tax administration may also access bank information directly where the taxpayer unlawfully obstructed or hindered the tax administration from access to documents supporting the accounting records when the taxpayer is subject to organised accounting for tax purposes or to verify the granting of tax benefits. Access to bank information is also possible when the tax administration does not have the possibility of directly verifying the taxable income, where the declared income in respect of the personal income tax is under some average or in order to confirm the use of public funds.
Russian Federation	Yes	No	N/A	N/A	No	
Saint Kitts and Nevis	No	No	Yes*	Affirmative action, the likely effect of which was to mislead or conceal (e.g. keeping a double set of books, making false entries or alterations to financial records).	No	*Pursuant to anti-money laundering law and MLAT with the United States.
Saint Lucia	No*	No	Yes**	Wilful action with the intent to evade assessment or liability to tax.	No	*The TIEA with the United States does not extend to activities in the offshore sector. **With respect to Commonwealth countries and the United States.

Table B.2 Access to Bank Information for Exchange of Information Purposes

1	2	3	4	5	6	7
Country	Ability to obtain bank info for EOI purposes in all tax matters	Ability to obtain bank info for EOI purposes in all tax matters only if domestic tax interest present	Ability to obtain bank info for EOI purposes only in criminal tax matters	If ability restricted to criminal tax matters, standard used to determine "criminal tax matters"	Inability to obtain bank information for any tax information exchange purposes	Notes/Other
Saint Vincent and the Grenadines	No*	N/A	Yes	Dual criminality applies. Criminal conduct is drug trafficking or a relevant offence under the anti-money laundering legislation. Relevant offence is defined in the Proceeds of Crime Money Laundering Prevention Act and its amendments to include summary and indictable offences.	No	*Information gathering powers adopted to implement the CARICOM tax treaty do not extend to information in the offshore sector.
Samoa	No	No	Yes	See Tables A2 and A5.		
San Marino	No	No	Yes	See Table A2	No	
Seychelles	Yes	No	N/A	N/A	No	
Singapore	No	Yes	N/A	N/A	No	
Slovak Republic	Yes	No	N/A	N/A	No	
South Africa	Yes	No	N/A	N/A	No	
Spain	Yes	No	N/A	N/A	No	
Sweden	Yes	No	N/A	N/A	No	
Switzerland	No	No	Yes	See Table A5	No	
Turkey	Yes	No	N/A	N/A	No	
Turks and Caicos Islands	No	N/A	Yes*	See Table A5.	No	*With respect to the MLAT with the United States.
United Arab Emirates	Yes	No	N/A	N/A	No	

Table B.2 Access to Bank Information for Exchange of Information Purposes

1	2	3	4	5	6	7
Country	Ability to obtain bank info for EOI purposes in all tax matters	Ability to obtain bank info for EOI purposes in all tax matters only if domestic tax interest present	Ability to obtain bank info for EOI purposes only in criminal tax matters	If ability restricted to criminal tax matters, standard used to determine "criminal tax matters"	Inability to obtain bank information for any tax information exchange purposes	Notes/Other
United Kingdom	Yes	No	N/A	N/A	No	
United States	Yes	No	N/A	N/A	No	
United States Virgin Islands	Yes	No	N/A	N/A	No	
Uruguay	No	No	Yes*	Dual criminality only applies to the extent that exchange is requested in relation to a crime that would not generally be considered a criminal offence. Tax evasion involving an intentional act or omission such as a failure to report income that should be reported to tax authorities or the falsification of information or documents, including a tax return, in order to reduce a tax liability that was otherwise due, would not be protected from exchange by a dual criminality requirement.	No	*Application must be made to the Criminal Court.
Vanuatu	No	N/A	Yes*	See Table A5.	No	*On a discretionary basis. (See Table A2).

Table B.3
Procedures to obtain bank information for exchange of information purposes

Explanation of columns 2 through 4

Table B3 shows for each of the countries reviewed whether the country's competent authority has the power to obtain bank information directly or if separate authorisation is required (**column 2**). **Column 3** indicates whether a country has measures in place to compel the production of information if a bank refuses to provide information to the country's authorities. Additional explanatory comments for some countries are found in **column 4**.

Table B.3   Procedures to obtain bank information for exchange of information purposes

1	2	3	4
Country	Competent authority has direct access to bank information and does not need separate authorization	Measures to compel production of bank information	Notes / Other
Andorra	No. Decision by the Magistracy whether the request for information fulfils the conditions for admission under the agreement with the European Communities or the International Criminal Co-operation Law.*	Yes	*Information can be obtained in matters related to tax fraud in the case of savings income. (See Table B2).
Anguilla	Yes*	Yes**	*Access relates to the savings agreements with the EU Member States and the MLAT with the United States. (See Table B2). **With respect to the MLAT with the United States.
Antigua and Barbuda	Yes*	Yes	*In connection with the TIEA with the United States.
Argentina	Yes*	Yes	*The competent authority is not the tax administration when the exchange of information is carried out through DTCs, but the tax administration has direct access to bank information in these cases.
Aruba	Yes*	Yes	*In connection with a DTC or TIEA.
Australia	Yes*	Yes	*In connection with a DTC or TIEA.
Austria	Yes*	Yes	*In connection with a DTC or TIEA.
The Bahamas	Yes*	Yes*	*In connection with the TIEA with the United States.
Bahrain	Yes*	Yes	*The procedure depends on the context within which information is sought. (See Table B2).
Barbados	Yes*	Yes	*In connection with a DTC or TIEA.
Belgium	Yes	Yes	The civil servant appointed by the Minister of Finance, can lift bank secrecy in cases where a tax fraud or preparation of a tax fraud is presumed. Further, when a taxpayer challenges a tax adjustment the tax inspector may require a banking institution to provide any information at its disposal that may be useful for investigating the challenge.
Belize	No. Court order is required.	Yes	
Bermuda	Yes*	Yes	*In connection with a DTC or TIEA. In relation to other countries, a court order is required.
British Virgin Islands	Yes*	Yes	*In connection with a TIEA and an MLAT. The Competent authority for a TIEA is the Financial Secretary and for an MLAT the Attorney General.

Table B.3 Procedures to obtain bank information for exchange of information purposes

1	2	3	4
Country	Competent authority has direct access to bank information and does not need separate authorization	Measures to compel production of bank information	Notes / Other
Brunei	No information.	No information.	
Canada	Yes*	Yes	*In connection with a DTC or TIEA. In other cases separate authorization may be required.
Cayman Islands	Yes*	Yes	*In connection with a DTC or TIEA. In other cases authorisation may be required.
China	Yes.*Approval by director of the tax department is required.	Yes	*In connection with a DTC or TIEA.
Cook Islands	Yes. Authorisation by the Attorney General for the taking of evidence.*	Yes	*Under the Mutual Assistance in Criminal Matters Act (MACMA) 2003.
Costa Rica	No. Court order required.	Yes	
Cyprus	No. Court order required.**	Yes	*A court order is not necessary to obtain information from banking institutions for the implementation of the EU Savings Directive.
Czech Republic	Yes*	Yes	*In connection with a DTC or MLAT. In other cases, e.g. European Convention on Mutual Assistance in Criminal Matters, separate authorization may be required.
Denmark	Yes*	Yes	*In connection with a DTC or MLAT. In other cases separate authorization may be required.
Dominica	No information.	No information.	
Finland	Yes*	Yes	*In connection with a DTC or TIEA.
France	Yes*	Yes	*In connection with a DTC or TIEA. In other cases separate authorization may be required.
Germany	Yes	Yes	*In connection with a DTC or TIEA. In other cases separate authorization may be required.
Gibraltar	N/A*	N/A*	*Gibraltar has no powers to obtain information from banks and financial institutions. However, the competent authority receives the necessary information to carry out its obligations under the EU Savings Directive (See Table B2).
Greece	No. Court order required.	Yes	
Grenada	No information.	No information.	

Table B.3   Procedures to obtain bank information for exchange of information purposes

1	2	3	4
Country	Competent authority has direct access to bank information and does not need separate authorization	Measures to compel production of bank information	Notes / Other
Guatemala	N/A*	N/A*	*No exchange of information for tax purposes.
Guernsey	Yes*	Yes	*In connection with a TIEA. Otherwise the approach to be followed in obtaining bank information depends on the particular assistance arrangements under which information is sought. Authorization by the Attorney General or judicial authorities may be required.
Hong Kong, China	Yes	Yes	
Hungary	Yes*	Yes	*In connection with a DTC or TIEA.
Iceland	Yes*	Yes	*In connection with a DTC or TIEA.
Ireland	Yes. The consent of a Revenue Commissioner is required to issue a notice seeking information from a financial institution.*	Yes	*In connection with a DTC or TIEA. In other cases separate authorization may be required, e.g. from a court.
Isle of Man	Yes*	Yes	*In connection with a TIEA or a new DTC. Otherwise the approach to be followed in obtaining bank information depends on the particular assistance arrangements under which information is sought, e.g. Attorney General's authorisation in some cases.
Italy	Yes, upon ex-ante authorisation by the Director of the Central Assessment Department or of the competent Regional Department of the Revenue Agency, or by the Regional Commanding Officer of the Guardia di Finanza. No authorisation is required for complementary requests.	Yes	
Japan	Yes.*With the authorisation of the District Director of the Tax Office.	Yes	*In connection with a DTC.
Jersey	Yes*	Yes	*In connection with a TIEA. Otherwise the approach to be followed in obtaining bank information depends on the particular assistance arrangements, under which information is sought, e.g. Attorney General's authorisation in some cases.
Korea	Yes*	Yes	*In connection with a DTC. In other cases separate authorisation may be required.
Liechtenstein	No. Court order required.*	Yes	*In connection with the MLAT with the United States and the Savings Agreement with the European Communities.

Table B.3 Procedures to obtain bank information for exchange of information purposes

1	2	3	4
Country	Competent authority has direct access to bank information and does not need separate authorization	Measures to compel production of bank information	Notes / Other
Luxembourg	No. Court order required.	Yes	
Macao, China	No. Court order required.	Yes	
Malaysia	No*		*Tax authorities do not have direct access to information held by banks in civil tax matters but can obtain bank information from the taxpayer where there is a domestic tax interest.
Malta	Yes	Yes	
Marshall Islands	Yes*	Yes	*In connection with the TIEA with the United States.
Mauritius	Yes*	Yes	*Where the Commissioner does not have power to obtain bank information under the Income Tax Act he would have to apply to a Judge in Chambers for an order of disclosure.
Mexico	No. Information can be obtained through the National Banking and Insurance Commission.	Yes	
Monaco	Yes*	Yes	*In connection with a) the treaty with France, b) EU Savings Agreement for criminal offences, and c) VAT regarding all EU Member States.
Montserrat	Yes*	No information.	*Access relates to the savings agreements with the EU Member States and the MLAT with the United States. (See Table B2). The competent authority for the purposes of the MLAT is the Attorney General.
Nauru	N/A*	N/A*	*Nauru's laws do not provide access to bank information for tax purposes.
Netherlands	Yes*	Yes	*In connection with a DTC or TIEA.
Netherlands Antilles	Yes	Yes	
New Zealand	Yes*	Yes	*In connection with a DTC or TIEA.
Niue	Yes.*	Yes	*In connection with a request under the Mutual Assistance in Criminal Matters Act (MACMA). The competent authority for the purposes of the MACMA is the Attorney General.
Norway	Yes*	Yes	*In connection with a DTC or TIEA.
Panama	N/A*	N/A*	*No exchange of information in tax matters other than in connection with certain criminal offences under the MLAT with the United States (See Table A5).

Table B.3   Procedures to obtain bank information for exchange of information purposes

1	2	3	4
Country	Competent authority has direct access to bank information and does not need separate authorization	Measures to compel production of bank information	Notes / Other
Philippines	Yes*	Yes*	*With respect to information held by financial institutions other than banks. The Commissioner of Inland Revenue does not have power to obtain information held by banks, except for the limited purposes described in Table B2.
Poland	Yes. Request from the head of a revenue office or the head of a customs office in the form of a ruling.*	Yes	*In connection with a DTC or TIEA.
Portugal	Yes. In some cases judicial authorisation is required.*	Yes	*Access to bank information when there are reasonable grounds to believe that a tax crime has been committed or where there are concrete identified facts that a person provided false information to the tax administration does not depend on a judicial authorisation. However, an audit of the taxpayer is required and judicial appeal is possible. In all cases, tax administration decisions to access protected bank information must be based on real and justified facts. Those decisions are taken at the level of Director-General and may not be delegated.
Russian Federation	Yes	Yes	
Saint Kitts and Nevis	No, access through Financial Intelligence Unit.	Yes	
Saint Lucia	No. Court order.*	Yes	*Mutual legal assistance procedures.
Saint Vincent and the Grenadines	No, access through Financial Intelligence Unit.*	Yes	*The approach to be followed in obtaining information depends on the use for which the information is being requested. A court order is required in cases where the information is requested for evidentiary purposes in court.
Samoa	No. Court order required.	Yes	
San Marino	No. Court order required.*	Yes	*In relation to the Savings Agreement with the European Communities, the Body responsible for EU taxation may rely on the Central Bank (and offices of the Public Administration) for relevant information.
Seychelles	Yes*	Yes	*In connection with a request under Mutual Assistance in Criminal Matters Act (MACMA) the Attorney General is the competent authority.
Singapore	Yes*	Yes	*In connection with a DTC or TIEA.
Slovak Republic	Yes*	Yes	*In connection with a DTC or TIEA.
South Africa	Yes*	Yes	*In connection with a DTC or TIEA.
Spain	Yes*	Yes	*In connection with a DTC or TIEA.

Table B.3   Procedures to obtain bank information for exchange of information purposes

1	2	3	4
Country	Competent authority has direct access to bank information and does not need separate authorization	Measures to compel production of bank information	Notes / Other
Sweden	Yes*	Yes	*In connection with a DTC or TIEA.
Switzerland	Yes*	Yes	*The procedures and competences differ depending on whether bank information is provided pursuant to a DTC (competence: Federal Tax Administration) or pursuant to the mutual assistance law or treaties (competence: cantonal judicial authorities/ Federal Office of Justice).
Turkey	Yes*	Yes	*In connection with a DTC or TIEA.
Turks and Caicos Islands	No. Judicial procedures.*	Yes	*In connection with the MLAT with the United States.
United Arab Emirates	Yes*	Yes*	*In connection with a DTC.
United Kingdom	No. The consent of an independent Commissioner is required.*	Yes	*In connection with a DTC or TIEA. In other cases judicial authorisation may be required.
United States	Yes*	Yes	*In connection with a DTC or TIEA.
United States Virgin Islands	Yes*	Yes	*In connection with a DTC or TIEA.
Uruguay	No. Application must be made to the Criminal Court to lift banking secrecy.	Yes	
Vanuatu	Yes.*	Yes	*In connection with a request under the Mutual Assistance in Criminal Matters Act (MACMA). The competent authority for the purposes of the MACMA is the Attorney General.

C.   Access to Ownership, Identity and Accounting Information

Table C.1
Information Gathering Powers

This table gives an overview of the information gathering powers available to the authorities in each of the countries reviewed to obtain information in response to a request for exchange of information for tax purposes.

Explanation of columns 2 through 6.

Column 2 shows which countries have powers to obtain information required to be kept by a person subject to record keeping obligations (e.g. as a taxpayer). The column is divided into two sub-columns that show whether countries can obtain information in connection with a request for information in civil and criminal tax matters respectively.

Column 3 shows which countries have powers to obtain information from persons not required to keep such information. The column is divided into two sub-columns that show whether countries can obtain information in connection with a request for information in civil and criminal tax matters respectively.

Column 4 indicates if powers may only be used if the country has an interest in the information for its own tax purposes (domestic tax interest).

Column 5 indicates whether a country has measures in place to compel production of information.

Column 6 includes explanatory comments.

Table C.1   Information Gathering Powers

1	2		3		4	5	6
Country	Powers to obtain information for EOI purposes				These powers may only be used where a domestic tax interest exists	Measures to compel production of information	Notes
	Information required to be kept		Information not required to be kept				
	Civil	Criminal	Civil	Criminal			
Andorra	No	Yes*	No	Yes*	No	Yes	*Powers to obtain information apply in the context of tax fraud in relation to savings income paid to EU resident individuals. (See Table B2).
Anguilla	No*	Yes**	No	Yes**	No	Yes**	*Anguilla can obtain information with respect to savings income exchanged automatically under the bilateral agreements with the EU Member States. (See Table A2). **Anguilla can obtain information requested under the MLAT with the United States in certain criminal tax matters. (See Table A5).
Antigua and Barbuda	Yes*	Yes*	Yes*	Yes*	No	Yes	*Pursuant to requests under TIEA with the United States.
Argentina	Yes	Yes	Yes	Yes	No	Yes	
Aruba	Yes	Yes	Yes	Yes	No	Yes	
Australia	Yes	Yes	Yes	Yes	No	Yes	
Austria	Yes*	Yes	Yes*	Yes	No	Yes	*Access to bank information is restricted to cases of tax evasion. (See Table B2).
The Bahamas	Yes*	Yes*	Yes*	Yes*	No	Yes	*The Bahamas has the power to obtain information needed to fulfil its obligations under its TIEA with the United States.
Bahrain	Yes*	Yes	Yes*	Yes	No	Yes	*The procedure and powers depend on the context within which information is sought. Information requested under a DTC can be obtained also for civil tax purposes. A request for information under the anti-money laundering law only covers criminal tax evasion.

Table C.1   Information Gathering Powers

1	2		3		4	5	6
Country	Powers to obtain information for EOI purposes				These powers may only be used where a domestic tax interest exists	Measures to compel production of information	Notes
	Information required to be kept		Information not required to be kept				
	Civil	Criminal	Civil	Criminal			
Barbados	Yes*	Yes	Yes*	Yes	No	Yes	*In Barbados some laws restrict information only to the domestic tax authorities. Barbados does not exchange information on low tax entities that are excluded from the scope of its tax treaties. These laws, however, can be overridden by a DTC and TIEA.
Belgium	Yes*	Yes	Yes*	Yes	No	Yes	*Access to bank information is restricted in certain civil tax matters. (See Table B2). However, the tax administration can obtain all information on the taxpayer's bank accounts from the taxpayer himself, insofar as these accounts are used by the taxpayer within the framework of his professional activity.
Belize	Yes*	Yes	Yes*	Yes	No	Yes, in criminal tax matters	*Access to bank information is restricted to criminal tax matters (See Table B2).
Bermuda	Yes*	Yes	Yes*	Yes	No	Yes	*With respect to requests from countries with which Bermuda has signed a TIEA. In relation to other countries Bermuda can obtain information for tax information exchange purposes in criminal tax matters.
British Virgin Islands	Yes*	Yes*	Yes*	Yes*	No	Yes	*The competent authority has power to obtain information needed to respond to a request for exchange of information where an exchange of information agreement such as a TIEA is in place.
Brunei	No information.	No information.	No information.	No information.	No information.	No information.	
Canada	Yes	Yes	Yes	Yes	No	Yes	

Table C.1   Information Gathering Powers

1	2		3		4	5	6
Country	Powers to obtain information for EOI purposes				These powers may only be used where a domestic tax interest exists	Measures to compel production of information	Notes
	Information required to be kept		Information not required to be kept				
	Civil	Criminal	Civil	Criminal			
Cayman Islands	Yes*	Yes*	Yes*	Yes*	No	Yes	*The Tax Information Authority has power to obtain information to respond to a request for exchange of information where an exchange of information agreement such as TIEA is in place.
China	Yes	Yes	Yes	Yes	No	Yes	
Cook Islands	No	Yes*	No	Yes*	No	Yes	*See Table A5.
Costa Rica	Yes*	Yes*	Yes*	Yes*	No	Yes	*Under the TIEA with the United States.
Cyprus	Yes*	Yes	No	No	Yes	No information.	*Limited access to bank information. (See Table B2) and access to information on international trusts only on the basis of a court order.
Czech Republic	Yes	Yes	Yes	Yes	No	Yes	
Denmark	Yes	Yes	Yes	Yes	No	Yes*	*No sanction to party unrelated to the tax matter if the unrelated party is not required to keep the information.
Dominica	Yes*	Yes*	No information.	No information.	No information.	No information.	*Information gathering powers limited to exchange in relation to activities in the onshore sector.
Finland	Yes	Yes	Yes	Yes	No	Yes	
France	Yes	Yes	Yes	Yes	No	Yes	
Germany	Yes	Yes	Yes	Yes	No	Yes	
Gibraltar	No*	No*	No	No	No	No*	*Gibraltar has enacted legislation to obtain the information needed to permit automatic exchange of information on interest income with the EU Member States in accordance with the EU Savings Directive.

Table C.1   Information Gathering Powers

1	2		3		4	5	6
Country	Powers to obtain information for EOI purposes				These powers may only be used where a domestic tax interest exists	Measures to compel production of information	Notes
	Information required to be kept		Information not required to be kept				
	Civil	Criminal	Civil	Criminal			
Greece	Yes	Yes	Yes	Yes	No	Yes	
Grenada	Yes*	Yes*	Yes*	Yes*	No	Yes	*Under the TIEA with the United States.
Guatemala	No*	No*	No*	No*	N/A*	N/A*	*Guatemala does not currently exchange information in tax matters with any country.
Guernsey	Yes*	Yes**	Yes*	Yes**	No	Yes	*The Tax Law provides the necessary powers to obtain information for tax purposes for EOI purposes under a TIEA. **Guernsey can obtain information for tax information exchange purposes in criminal tax matters in the absence of a TIEA or DTC.
Hong Kong, China	Yes	Yes	Yes	Yes	Yes	Yes	
Hungary	Yes	Yes	Yes*	Yes*	No	Yes	*Only if the tax authority investigates the taxpayer defined in a request for exchange of information and the control procedure is expanded to other taxpayers in contractual relationship with him.
Iceland	Yes	Yes	No	No	No	N/A	
Ireland	Yes	Yes	Yes	Yes	No	Yes	
Isle of Man	Yes*	Yes**	Yes*	Yes**	No	Yes	*Information powers are in place to meet obligations to exchange information in the context of a TIEA or a new DTC. **In the absence of a TIEA or DTC the Isle of Man can obtain information for tax information exchange purposes in criminal tax matters.
Italy	Yes	Yes	Yes	Yes	No	Yes	
Japan	Yes	Yes	Yes	Yes	No	Yes	

Table C.1   Information Gathering Powers

1	2		3		4	5	6
Country	Powers to obtain information for EOI purposes				These powers may only be used where a domestic tax interest exists	Measures to compel production of information	Notes
	Information required to be kept		Information <u>not</u> required to be kept				
	Civil	Criminal	Civil	Criminal			
Jersey	Yes*	Yes**	Yes*	Yes**	No	Yes	*Regulations have been enacted which enable Jersey to meet its obligations under the TIEA with the United States. **Notwithstanding the absence of a TIEA or DTC, for all countries, Jersey can obtain information for tax information exchange purposes in criminal tax matters.
Korea	Yes	Yes	Yes	Yes	No	Yes	
Liechten-stein	No	Yes*	No	Yes*	No	Yes*	*With respect to the MLAT with the United States and interest income paid to individuals resident in EU Member States. However, information registered with the Public Register is available freely and without any formality.
Luxem-bourg	Yes*	Yes	Yes	Yes	No	Yes	*Restrictions apply in relation to banking information (see Table B2) and in relation to 1929 Holding Companies.
Macao, China	Yes*	Yes	No	Yes**	No	Yes	*Restrictions apply to banking information. **Information that is not compulsorily held must be obtained by judicial order.
Malta	Yes*	Yes	Yes*	Yes	No	Yes	*Restrictions apply to banking information. (See Table B2).
Malaysia	Yes*	Yes**.	Yes*	Yes**	Yes	No information.	*Information powers do not override secrecy provisions in the various laws applicable in Labuan. **It is unclear if information can be obtained in criminal tax matters in the case of Labuan.

Table C.1   Information Gathering Powers

1	2		3		4	5	6
Country	Powers to obtain information for EOI purposes				These powers may only be used where a domestic tax interest exists	Measures to compel production of information	Notes
	Information required to be kept		Information not required to be kept				
	Civil	Criminal	Civil	Criminal			
Marshall Islands	Yes*	Yes*	Yes*	Yes*	No	Yes	*With respect to the TIEA with the United States. In other cases, only in criminal tax matters on a discretionary basis. (See Table A2).
Mauritius	Yes	Yes	Yes	Yes	No	Yes	
Mexico	Yes	Yes	Yes	Yes	No	Yes	
Monaco	Yes*	Yes	Yes*	Yes	No	Yes**	*Only with respect to France. **The Monaco tax authorities have access to any information on taxpayers established or resident in Monaco.
Montserrat	No*	Yes**	No*	Yes**	No	Yes	*Montserrat can obtain information with respect to savings income exchanged automatically under savings tax agreements with EU Member States. (See Table B2). **Only with respect to the United States in certain criminal tax matters.
Nauru	N/A*	N/A*	N/A*	N/A*	N/A*	N/A*	*Has no powers to obtain information in response to a request for exchange of information and no exchange of information arrangements in place.
Netherlands	Yes	Yes	Yes	Yes	No	Yes	
Netherlands Antilles	Yes	Yes	Yes	Yes	No	Yes	
New Zealand	Yes	Yes	Yes	Yes	No	Yes	
Niue	No	Yes*	No	Yes*	No	Yes*	*Provision of assistance in criminal tax matters, on a discretionary basis. (See Table A5).
Norway	Yes	Yes	Yes	Yes	No	Yes	

Table C.1   Information Gathering Powers

1	2		3		4	5	6
Country	Powers to obtain information for EOI purposes				These powers may only be used where a domestic tax interest exists	Measures to compel production of information	Notes
	Information required to be kept		Information not required to be kept				
	Civil	Criminal	Civil	Criminal			
Panama	No	No*	No	No*	N/A	N/A	*Panama has powers to obtain information for domestic tax purposes, but not for exchange purposes. The MLAT with the United States allows for information exchange in connection with certain criminal offences. (See Table A5).
Philippines	Yes*	Yes*	Yes*	Yes*	Yes	Yes	*Limited access to bank information. (See Table B2).
Poland	Yes	Yes	No information.	No information.	No	No information.	
Portugal	Yes*	Yes	Yes*	Yes	No	Yes	*Special provisions with respect to bank secrecy. (See Table B2).
Russian Federation	Yes	Yes	No	No	No	Yes	
Saint Kitts and Nevis	Yes	Yes	Yes	Yes	No	Yes	
Saint Lucia	Yes*	Yes**	No	Yes**	No	Yes	*Domestic information gathering powers limited to activities in the onshore sector. **In relation to Commonwealth countries and the United States.
Saint Vincent and Grenadines	No	Yes	No	Yes	No	Yes	
Samoa	No	Yes	No	Yes	No	Yes	
San Marino	Yes*	Yes	No	Yes**	No	Yes	*The competent authority can obtain information for the purposes of exchange of information arrangements. Restrictions apply to bank information. **See Table A2.
Seychelles	Yes	Yes	Yes	Yes	No	Yes	
Singapore	Yes	Yes	Yes	Yes	Yes	Yes	

Table C.1   Information Gathering Powers

1	2		3		4	5	6
Country	Powers to obtain information for EOI purposes				These powers may only be used where a domestic tax interest exists	Measures to compel production of information	Notes
	Information required to be kept		Information not required to be kept				
	Civil	Criminal	Civil	Criminal			
Slovak Republic	Yes	Yes	Yes	Yes	No	Yes	
South Africa	Yes	Yes	Yes	Yes	No	Yes	
Spain	Yes	Yes	Yes	Yes	No	Yes	
Sweden	Yes	Yes	Yes	Yes	No	Yes	
Switzerland	Yes*	Yes	No	Yes	No	Yes	*No access to bank information in civil tax matters. (See Table B2).
Turkey	Yes	Yes	Yes	Yes	No	Yes	
Turks & Caicos Islands	No	Yes*	No	No	N/A	Yes	*With respect to the United States in certain criminal tax matters. (See Table A2).
United Arab Emirates	Yes	Yes	Yes	Yes	No	Yes	
United Kingdom	Yes	Yes	Yes	Yes	No	Yes	
United States	Yes	Yes	Yes	Yes	No	Yes	
United States Virgin Islands	Yes	Yes	Yes	Yes	No	Yes	
Uruguay	Yes*	Yes	Yes*	Yes	No	Yes	*Access to bank information is restricted to criminal tax matters. (See Table B2).
Vanuatu	No	Yes*	No	Yes*	N/A	Yes	*See Table A5.

Table C.2
Statutory Confidentiality or Secrecy Provisions

This table shows the countries that have specific confidentiality or secrecy provisions relating to the disclosure of ownership, identity or accounting information. Where such provisions exist, the table notes whether the provisions are of a general or a specific nature and whether they are overridden if a request is made pursuant to an "EOI arrangement." An "EOI arrangement" includes any mechanism that permits information exchange for tax purposes with another country (*e.g.* DTC, MLAT, domestic law on mutual assistance in criminal matters).

Explanation of columns 2 through 6

Column 2 indicates whether the countries surveyed have statutory confidentiality or secrecy provisions applicable to ownership, identity and accounting information. If the answer is yes, **column 3** indicates whether those provisions apply generally in the country or are limited to specific entities (*e.g.* foundations) or sectors (*e.g.* banking or insurance).

Column 4 indicates whether the statutory confidentiality or secrecy provisions can be overridden if a request for information is made pursuant to an exchange of information arrangement. If the answer is yes, **column 5** (Notes) briefly outlines in what circumstances the secrecy or confidentiality provisions may be overridden.

Table C.2   Statutory Confidentiality or Secrecy Provision

1	2	3	4	5
Country	Statutory confidentiality or secrecy provisions prohibiting or restricting disclosure of ownership, identity or accounting information	Provisions of general application or specific to entities arrangements in particular sectors	Provision overridden if request for information is made pursuant to EOI arrangement	Notes
Andorra	Yes	General application.	N/A*	*No EOI arrangements other than those with the EU relating to tax fraud in the case of savings income.
Anguilla	Yes	Both general and specific provisions.	Yes*	*Can exchange information under the MLAT with the United States in certain criminal tax matters.
Antigua and Barbuda	Yes	Specific provisions.	Yes	
Aruba	No	N/A	N/A	
Argentina	No	N/A	N/A	
Australia	No	N/A	N/A	
Austria	No	N/A	N/A	
Bahamas	Yes	General application.	Yes*	*In connection with TIEA with the United States.
Bahrain	Yes	Specific provisions (financial trusts)	Yes	
Barbados	Yes (but not in cases of domestic entities).	Specific provisions.	Yes*	*However, Barbados does not exchange information on low tax entities that are excluded from the scope of its tax treaties.
Belgium	No	N/A	N/A	
Belize	No	N/A	N/A	
Bermuda	No	N/A	N/A	
British Virgin Islands	Yes	Specific provisions.	Yes	
Brunei	Yes	Specific provisions.	No information.	
Canada	No	N/A	N/A	
Cayman Islands	Yes	General application.	Yes	
China	No	N/A	N/A	
Cook Islands	Yes	Specific provisions.	Yes*	*In connection with a request under the Mutual Assistance in Criminal Matters Act.
Costa Rica	No	N/A	N/A	

Table C.2 Statutory Confidentiality or Secrecy Provision

1	2	3	4	5
Country	Statutory confidentiality or secrecy provisions prohibiting or restricting disclosure of ownership, identity or accounting information	Provisions of general application or specific to entities arrangements in particular sectors	Provision overridden if request for information is made pursuant to EOI arrangement	Notes
Cyprus	Yes	Specific provision (international trusts).	No*	*Subject to the terms of the instrument creating an international trust and if the court does not issue an order for disclosure the trustee or any other person cannot disclose information to anyone who has no right by law to know documents or information concerning the settlor, beneficiaries, trustees and their duties or accounts or property of the trust.
Czech Republic	No	N/A	N/A	
Denmark	No	N/A	N/A	
Dominica	No information.	No information.	No information.	
Finland	No	N/A	N/A	
France	No	N/A	N/A	
Germany	No	N/A	N/A	
Gibraltar	Yes	Specific provisions.*	No	*Provisions apply to exempt companies only. These companies will be phased out by 2010.
Greece	No	N/A	N/A	
Grenada	Yes	Specific provisions.	Yes*	*In connection with the Caricom tax treaty and the TIEA with the United States in relation to activities in the onshore sector.
Guatemala	Yes	General application.	N/A*	*No EOI arrangements.
Guernsey	No	N/A	N/A	
Hong Kong, China	No	N/A	N/A	
Hungary	No	N/A	N/A	
Iceland	No	N/A	N/A	
Ireland	No	N/A	N/A	
Isle of Man	No	N/A	N/A	
Italy	No	N/A	N/A	
Japan	No	N/A	N/A	
Jersey	No	N/A	N/A	
Korea	No	N/A	N/A	

Table C.2   Statutory Confidentiality or Secrecy Provision

1	2	3	4	5
Country	Statutory confidentiality or secrecy provisions prohibiting or restricting disclosure of ownership, identity or accounting information	Provisions of general application or specific to entities arrangements in particular sectors	Provision overridden if request for information is made pursuant to EOI arrangement	Notes
Liechtenstein	Yes	General application.	Yes*	*Secrecy provisions do not apply in connection with a request pursuant to the MLAT with the United States.
Luxembourg	No	N/A	N/A	
Macao, China	Yes	Specific provisions.	Yes	
Malaysia	Yes *	Specific provisions.	No	*Secrecy provisions contained in laws applicable in Labuan.
Malta	Yes	General application.	Yes*	*Where an EOI request is made under a DTC and the request relates to tax fraud any provision that restricts access to information from any of the following persons does not apply: licensed banks, licensed life insurance companies, persons licensed to carry on investment business, licensed investment schemes, and licensed stockbrokers.
Marshall Islands	No	N/A	N/A	
Mauritius	Yes	Specific provision.*	Yes	Confidentiality / secrecy does not affect the obligation of Mauritius or any Public Sector Agency under an international agreement.
Mexico	Yes*	Specific provision.**	No***	*Only financial institutions may act as trustees of domestic trusts and strict secrecy provisions prohibit them from disclosing information on beneficiaries and settlors, even to authorities. **Applies to all trustees of domestic trusts. ***Only as far as trusts are concerned.
Monaco	No	N/A	N/A	
Montserrat	Yes	Both general and specific provisions.	Yes*	*In connection with the MLAT with the US in certain criminal tax matters.
Nauru	Yes	Specific provisions.	N/A*	*No EOI arrangements.
Netherlands	No	N/A	N/A	
Netherlands Antilles	No	N/A	N/A	
New Zealand	No	N/A	N/A	

Table C.2 Statutory Confidentiality or Secrecy Provision

1	2	3	4	5
Country	Statutory confidentiality or secrecy provisions prohibiting or restricting disclosure of ownership, identity or accounting information	Provisions of general application or specific to entities arrangements in particular sectors	Provision overridden if request for information is made pursuant to EOI arrangement	Notes
Niue	Yes	Specific provisions.	Yes	In connection with a request under the Mutual Assistance in Criminal Tax Matters Act.
Norway	No	N/A	N/A	
Panama	Yes	General application.	Unclear.	
Philippines	No	N/A	N/A	
Poland	No	N/A	N/A	
Portugal	No	N/A	N/A	
Russian Federation	No	N/A	N/A	
Saint Kitts and Nevis	Yes	Both general and specific provisions.	Yes*	*In connection with the Caricom tax treaty and domestic legislation providing for exchange of information in certain criminal tax matters.
Saint Lucia	Yes	Specific provisions.	Yes*	*In relation to Commonwealth countries and the US in certain criminal tax matters.
Saint Vincent and the Grenadines	Yes	Specific provisions.	Yes*	*In relation to Commonwealth countries and the US in certain criminal tax matters.
Samoa	Yes	Specific provisions.	Yes	
San Marino	No	N/A	N/A	
Seychelles	Yes	Specific provisions.	Yes*	*In connection with its DTCs in relation to activities in the onshore sector.
Singapore	Yes	Specific to trust companies.	Yes*	*In connection with (i) a request made under the Mutual Assistance in Criminal Matters Act, and (ii) an EOI request made under bilateral DTCs where there is an interest to investigate/prosecute a domestic tax offence.
Slovak Republic	No	N/A	N/A	
South Africa	No	N/A	N/A	
Spain	No	N/A	N/A	
Sweden	No	N/A	N/A	
Switzerland	Yes	General application.	Yes*	*Professional secrecy rules are overridden for a request relating to tax fraud.
Turkey	No	N/A	N/A	

Table C.2   Statutory Confidentiality or Secrecy Provision

1	2	3	4	5
Country	Statutory confidentiality or secrecy provisions prohibiting or restricting disclosure of ownership, identity or accounting information	Provisions of general application or specific to entities arrangements in particular sectors	Provision overridden if request for information is made pursuant to EOI arrangement	Notes
Turks & Caicos Islands	Yes	Both general and specific provisions.	Yes*	*Can exchange information under the MLAT with the United States in certain criminal tax matters.
United Arab Emirates	Yes	Specific provisions.*	Yes	* The Dubai International Financial Centre[1] has a Data Protection Law designed to facilitate the transfer of personal data to jurisdictions with adequate data protection regimes.
United Kingdom	No	N/A	N/A	
United States	No	N/A	N/A	
United States Virgin Islands	No	N/A	N/A	
Uruguay	No	N/A	N/A	
Vanuatu	Yes	Specific provisions.	Yes*	**In connection with a request under the Mutual Assistance in Criminal Matters Act.

[1] The Dubai International Financial Centre (DIFC) is a UAE Federal Financial Free Zone created pursuant to constitutional amendment and enabling federal legislation whereby the DIFC is granted a separate jurisdictional identity within the UAE along with a grant of authority to legislate for itself in the civil and commercial fields. The DIFC remains subject to compliance with UAE criminal law (including Anti-Money Laundering and Counter-terrorism Financing legislation) and UAE treaties and conventions. Although there are a number of free zones in the UAE, to date the DIFC is the only federally mandated free zone enjoying broad legislative and regulatory autonomy while remaining an integral part of the UAE.

Table C.3
Bearer Securities

Explanation of columns 2 through 6

Table C3 shows which of the countries reviewed allow for the issuance of bearer shares (**column 2**) and bearer debt (**column 4**). Where countries permit the issuance of such bearer instruments, the table outlines the measures adopted to identify owners of bearer shares (**column 3**) and bearer debt (**column 5**). The measures listed include both specific mechanisms, such as immobilisation procedures, ensuring that the owner is known in all cases as well as applicable anti-money laundering rules imposing a requirement on service providers in the financial sector to perform customer due diligence. Some explanatory comments are provided in **column 6**.

Table C.3   Bearer Securities

1	2	3	4	5	6
Country	Bearer shares may be issued	Mechanisms to identify owners of bearer shares	Bearer debt may be issued	Mechanisms to identify owners of bearer debt	Notes
Andorra	No	N/A	Yes*	Paying agents must establish the identity of individuals to whom interest is paid for the purposes of the agreement between Andorra and the European Communities in relation to the EU Savings Directive.[1] Further all financial institutions are subject to "know your customer" requirements under applicable anti-money laundering legislation.	*There are no specific laws regulating bearer debt.
Anguilla	Yes	No*	Yes	Paying agents must establish the identity of individuals to whom interest is paid for the purpose of the savings tax agreements with EU Member States.[2]	*Anguilla is planning to adopt legislation requiring the immobilisation of bearer shares.
Antigua and Barbuda	Yes	Bearer shares must be held by an approved custodian.	No information.	No information.	
Aruba	Yes	A combination of various regimes, Code of Commerce, Tax Law, Anti-Money Laundering Law effectively immobilize bearer shares or make their use impossible.	No	N/A	
Argentina	No	N/A	No	N/A	
Australia	No	N/A	Yes	Issuer of debentures required to identify holders or pay tax on interest at rate of 45%.	
Austria	Yes*	Shares are typically held in securities accounts and the holder of the security account is known. Anti-money laundering rules also provide a mechanism to identify owners of companies.[3]	Yes	Similar to mechanisms used for bearer shares. Further pursuant to legislation implementing the EU Savings Directive paying agents must establish the identity of individuals to whom interest is paid. [4]	*Joint stock companies.

Table C.3   Bearer Securities

1	2	3	4	5	6
Country	Bearer shares may be issued	Mechanisms to identify owners of bearer shares	Bearer debt may be issued	Mechanisms to identify owners of bearer debt	Notes
The Bahamas	No	N/A	Yes	All financial institutions and banks are required under applicable anti-money laundering legislation to conduct "know your customer" verifications on customers and clients and maintain records of such information.	
Bahrain	No	N/A	No	N/A	
Barbados	No	N/A	N/A	N/A	
Belgium	Yes	In order to vote, annual meetings of shareholders must be informed of the identity of owners of bearer shares. Further, there are circumstances in which a company has to provide information on the identity of shareholders to tax authorities. See also footnote 3.	Yes	See footnote 4.	Note that the law of the 14th of December 2005 prohibits the issuance of bearer securities as from 1 January 2008.
Belize	Yes	Bearer shares issued by IBCs incorporated after 2000 must be immobilised.	N/A	N/A	
Bermuda	No	N/A	Yes	Know your customer requirements imposed on regulated institutions which issue bearer debt would generally apply.	
British Virgin Islands	Yes	Bearer shares must be held by an approved / authorised custodian.*	Yes	See footnote 2	*Bearer shares held by companies incorporated prior to 1 January 2005 must be immobilised by 2010.
Brunei	No	N/A	No information.	No information.	
Canada	Yes	Investigative powers.*There are also provisions in corporate law which assist in identifying owners of bearer securities such as requirements for registration in order to vote, receive notices, interest dividends or other payments.	Yes	Investigative powers.* See also column 3.	*Refers to powers of the tax administration to require information to be provided.

Table C.3 Bearer Securities

1	2	3	4	5	6
Country	Bearer shares may be issued	Mechanisms to identify owners of bearer shares	Bearer debt may be issued	Mechanisms to identify owners of bearer debt	Notes
Cayman Islands	Yes	Entities doing relevant financial business are required to comply with the requirements of anti-money laundering provisions and pursuant to companies law bearer shares must be immobilised.	Yes	Investigative powers combined with "know your customer" rules arising under anti-money laundering laws where debt is issued in the Cayman Islands. See also footnote 2.	
China	Yes*	No	Yes*	No	*Allowed by Company Law, but have never been issued in practice.
Cook Islands	Yes	Bearer shares must be held by an approved custodian.	Yes	Bearer debt instruments must be held by an approved custodian.	
Costa Rica	Yes	Annual shareholder meeting must be informed of the identity of owners of bearer shares.	Yes	No	
Cyprus	Yes*	See footnote 3.*	No	N/A	*The International Collective Investment Schemes Law allows one type of scheme to issue bearer shares which designated to be marketed to the general public. However, this bearer share scheme will soon be abolished. No such public schemes have been approved.
Czech Republic	Yes	Ownership information on bearer shares in electronic form is recorded by a special centre. Holders of bearer shares in paper form may not participate at the annual shareholder meeting unless they disclose their identities. See also footnote 3.	Yes	Any securities that are filed in records are accessible in the same way as data covered by bank secrecy. See also footnote 4.	
Denmark	Yes	Investigative powers. See also footnote 3.	Yes	Investigative powers. See also footnote 4.	
Dominica	Yes	Bearer shares must be held by an approved custodian.	No information.	No information.	
Finland	No	N/A	Yes	Investigative powers. See also footnote 4.	
France	Yes	See footnote 3.	Yes	See footnote 4.	

Table C.3 Bearer Securities

1	2	3	4	5	6
Country	Bearer shares may be issued	Mechanisms to identify owners of bearer shares	Bearer debt may be issued	Mechanisms to identify owners of bearer debt	Notes
Germany	Yes*	Any shareholder that obtains more than 25 percent of the share capital must inform the AG. There is a separate disclosure obligation once a shareholder owns the majority of the company. For AG's traded on a stock exchange such reporting obligations exist once 5, 10, 25, 50, or 75 % of voting power has been reached. See also footnote 3.	Yes	Identity of owners of bearer debt can often be determined through custodians that hold the securities on behalf of their customers. Government offers investors in government bonds custodian services free of charge. See also column 3 and footnote 4.	*Stock companies (AG). Other corporate entities, in particular the Limited Liability Company (GmbH) cannot issue bearer shares.
Gibraltar	No	N/A	No	N/A	
Greece	No information.	No information (however, see footnote 3).	No information.	No information (however, see footnote 4).	
Grenada	Yes	Bearer shares must be held by an approved custodian.	No information.	No information.	
Guatemala	Yes	Not for tax purposes.	Yes	Not for tax purposes.	
Guernsey	No	N/A	Yes	Investigative powers combined with "know your customer" rules arising under Guernsey's anti-money laundering laws. See also footnote 2.	
Hong Kong, China	Yes*	The issue of bearer shares is required to be reflected in a company's register of members, which is available for public inspection. Financial institutions, such as banking, securities and insurance institutions are required under enforceable anti-money laundering guidelines to conduct customer due diligence and keep such record, including the record of beneficial owners, such as bearer share owners.	Yes	No	*Hong Kong, China is now rewriting its company law. In this exercise, it will consider whether the issue of bearer shares should still be permitted under its company law or not.
Hungary	No	N/A	No	N/A	
Iceland	No	N/A	No	N/A	

Table C.3   Bearer Securities

1	2	3	4	5	6
Country	Bearer shares may be issued	Mechanisms to identify owners of bearer shares	Bearer debt may be issued	Mechanisms to identify owners of bearer debt	Notes
Ireland	Yes*	Any person or group that acquires or disposes of any form of interest in shares of a public limited company that brings their shareholding above or below 5% of the issued share capital must notify the company. See also footnote 3.	Yes	See footnote 4.	*Public limited companies.
Isle of Man	No	N/A	No	N/A	
Italy	While formally provided for by the 1942 Civil Code, subsequent legislation prevents the issuing of bearer shares	N/A	Yes	See footnote 4.	
Japan	No	N/A	Yes	A payment record with identity information is submitted to the tax authorities depending on the amount of the redemption proceeds or the amount of annual interest.	
Jersey	No	N/A	Yes	Investigative powers in criminal matters combined with 'know your customer' rules arising under Jersey's anti-money laundering laws. See also footnote 2.	
Korea	Yes	Identity information deposited with the company.	Yes	Investigative powers.	
Liechtenstein	Yes	Liechtenstein anti-money laundering rules require that at least one person acting as an organ or director of a legal entity that does not conduct any commercial business in its country of domicile is obliged to identify and record the ultimate beneficial owner.	Yes*	See footnote 1.	*Bearer debts which safeguard mortgages in their function as securities.
Luxembourg	Yes	See footnote 3.	Yes	See footnote 4.	

Table C.3 Bearer Securities

1	2	3	4	5	6
Country	Bearer shares may be issued	Mechanisms to identify owners of bearer shares	Bearer debt may be issued	Mechanisms to identify owners of bearer debt	Notes
Macao, China	Yes	The new anti-money laundering legislation and the new administrative framework dealing with anti-money laundering require financial institutions to perform customer due diligence, including the identification of the owners of bearer shares.	Yes	No	
Malaysia	No information.	No information.	No information.	No information.	
Malta	No	N/A	Yes	Transfers of debts have to be executed in writing and ownership must be recorded in a Registrar of debentures ("debentures" includes all corporate debt instruments). See also footnote 3.	
Marshall Islands	Yes	No	No	N/A	
Mauritius	No	N/A	No	N/A	
Mexico	No	N/A	Yes	Investment companies are required to present a return regarding the withholding taxes record issued to a member of the group.	
Monaco	No*	N/A	Yes	Persons paying interest must report the identity of payee to tax authorities. See also footnote 1.	*Except for only two listed traded companies in which cases the shares must be held by a custodian.
Montserrat	Yes	Bearer shares must be held by an approved custodian.	Yes	Beneficial owner must be disclosed to the issuing financial institution. See also footnote 2.	
Nauru	Yes	No	Yes	No	
Netherlands	Yes	See footnote 3.	No	N/A	
Netherlands Antilles	Yes	Companies carrying out an activity requiring a license must disclose the beneficial owners to financial authorities.	Yes	Companies carrying out an activity requiring a license must disclose the beneficial owners to financial authorities. See also footnote 2.	
New Zealand	No	N/A	No	N/A	
Niue	Yes	No	No information.	No information.	

Table C.3   Bearer Securities

1	2	3	4	5	6
Country	**Bearer shares may be issued**	**Mechanisms to identify owners of bearer shares**	**Bearer debt may be issued**	**Mechanisms to identify owners of bearer debt**	**Notes**
Norway	No	N/A	Yes	The book-keeping Act requires businesses to record the counter-party of every transaction, which includes the issuance of bearer debt.	
Panama	Yes*	Regulations are in place requiring financial institutions, including trust companies, and registered agents to identify their clients and thus to identify the holders of registered and bearer shares.	Yes*	Unclear.	*Bearer shares and bearer debts have never been issued in practice in the Panamanian securities markets.
Philippines	No	N/A	No	N/A	
Poland	No information.	No information.	No information.	No information.	
Portugal	Yes	Income from bearer securities is subject to a withholding tax. Due to their "special nature", the owner is not identified unless some income is paid or when such securities are registered (for instance the shares of joint stock companies must be registered). Where income is paid the issuing company is required to keep an updated record of income owners, and the information is lodged each year with the tax authorities. See also footnote 2.	Yes	See column 3 and footnote 4.	
Russian Federation	No	N/A	Yes	No	
Saint Kitts and Nevis	Yes*	Bearer shares must be held by an approved custodian.	Yes	Beneficial owners must be disclosed to the issuing financial institution.	*In Nevis, domestic companies are not authorised to issue bearer shares or bearer share certificates.
Saint Lucia	No	N/A	No	N/A	
Saint Vincent and the Grenadines	Yes	Bearer shares must be held by an approved custodian.	No	N/A	
Samoa	Yes	No*	Yes	No*	*Samoa is planning to adopt legislation requiring the immobilisation of bearer instruments.

Table C.3 Bearer Securities

1	2	3	4	5	6
Country	Bearer shares may be issued	Mechanisms to identify owners of bearer shares	Bearer debt may be issued	Mechanisms to identify owners of bearer debt	Notes
San Marino	Yes	Under the law n° 130 which entered into force 11 December 2006 as from January 1 2008, the anonymous stock corporations' meetings must be held in presence of a notary public who has to identify the holder of bearer shares and keep the identity information for 5 years. Such information can be obtained only from judicial authority. Under the law n° 165 2005, if the company is a banking or other financial istitution, information on shareholders have to be reported to the Central Bank.	Yes	See footnote 1	
Seychelles	Yes	Yes. Mechanisms exist to identify the owners of bearer shares.*	No	N/A	*The IBC Act 1994 has been amended to provide that the names and addresses of persons to whom bearer shares are issued or transferred must be recorded in a register maintained by a service provider in the Seychelles or in the office of another intermediary or agent in another jurisdiction.
Singapore	No	N/A	No	N/A	
Slovak Republic	Yes	Bearer shares must have the form of book-entry securities. The central depository shall, among other things, register owners of book-entry securities in owner's accounts. Transfer of a security in book-entry form has to be registered by a central depository. See also footnote 3.	Yes	Only if bearer debts have the form of book-entry securities (bearer bonds must have the form of book-entry securities). The central depository shall, among other things, register owners of book-entry securities in owner's accounts. Transfer of a security in book-entry form has to be registered by a central depository. See also footnote 4.	

Table C.3   Bearer Securities

1	2	3	4	5	6
Country	Bearer shares may be issued	Mechanisms to identify owners of bearer shares	Bearer debt may be issued	Mechanisms to identify owners of bearer debt	Notes
South Africa	Yes (bearer share warrants)*	Investigative powers.**	Yes	Owners can only be identified at maturity or in the case of a debenture when name of holder is entered in register of debentures.	*Only public companies may issue bearer share warrants. Exchange control restrictions severely restrict their usefulness. **Refers to powers of tax administration to require information to be provided.
Spain	Yes	Transfers of non-publicly traded bearer shares must be undertaken by a financial institution, securities agency or a notary which must retain identity information. See also footnote 3.	Yes	See column 3 and footnote 4.	
Sweden	No	N/A	Yes	Taxpayers are required to disclose information to the tax authorities if it is necessary for tax assessment purposes. See also footnote 4. Information could in some cases be found in the accounting records.	
Switzerland	Yes	Owners of bearer shares must be disclosed to Swiss tax authorities if they apply for a refund or reduction of Swiss withholding tax. In connection with companies listed on a Swiss stock exchange, any holding of voting rights of 5% or more must be disclosed to the company and the stock exchange. Pursuant to Swiss anti-money laundering law, the organs, resident in Switzerland, of domiciliary companies are considered to be financial intermediaries and are therefore under the obligation to identify the beneficial owners.*	Yes	In case of interest paid by banks on bearer debt, the withholding tax gives the possibility to identify the owner if he requests a refund or reduction of Swiss withholding tax. See also footnote 1.	*A proposal is currently in the stage of public consultation pursuant to which holders of bearer shares who have more than 10% of the voting rights would have to identify themselves to the company if they wish to participate (vote) in a shareholders' meeting.
Turkey	Yes*	Bearer shares held in a central custody and settlement institution.	Yes	Bearer debt held in a central custody and settlement institution.	*Only public companies traded on the stock exchange.

Table C.3   Bearer Securities

1	2	3	4	5	6
Country	Bearer shares may be issued	Mechanisms to identify owners of bearer shares	Bearer debt may be issued	Mechanisms to identify owners of bearer debt	Notes
Turks & Caicos Islands	Yes	Bearer shares must be held by an approved custodian.	No	N/A	
United Arab Emirates	No	N/A	No	N/A	
United Kingdom	Yes	Persons holding bearer shares issued by public companies which are material and greater than 3% or greater than 10% must disclose such interests. See also footnote 1.	Yes	Where debt instruments are held in CREST, the UK securities settlement system and securities depository, CREST has to keep a record of ownership. See also footnote 4.	
United States	Yes	Investigative powers.	Yes	Investigative powers.	Corporations are formed under the laws of the several US States, the vast majority of which do not allow the issuance of bearer shares. More information is available at www.ustreas.gov/offices/enforcement/pdf/mlta.pdf.
United States Virgin Islands	No	N/A	Yes	Investigative powers.	
Uruguay	Yes	Annual shareholder meeting must be informed of the identity of owners of bearer shares that attend meetings.	Yes	No	
Vanuatu	Yes	No	Yes	No	

[1] Pursuant to agreements with the European Community providing for measures equivalent to those laid down in the Council Directive 2003/48/EC (Savings Tax Directive) Andorra, Liechtenstein, Monaco, San Marino and Switzerland have agreed procedures to be followed by paying agents established in those countries to establish the identity and residence of their customers (beneficial owners) who are individuals resident in EU Member States. Paying agents must identify beneficial owners of interest irrespective of whether a debt instrument is in registered or bearer form. Different obligations are placed on paying agents depending on whether contractual relations were entered into, or transactions were carried out in the absence of contractual relations, on or after 1 January 2004.

[2] The 27 Member States of the EU have entered into savings tax agreements with 10 associated and dependent territories: Anguilla, Aruba, British Virgin Islands, Cayman Islands, Guernsey, Isle of Man, Jersey, Montserrat, Netherlands Antilles and Turks and Caicos Islands. Pursuant to these agreements paying agents are required to establish the identity and residence of their customers (beneficial owners) who are individuals resident in EU Member States according to agreed procedures. Paying agents must identify beneficial owners of interest irrespective of whether a debt instrument is in registered or bearer form. Different obligations apply depending on whether contractual relations were entered into or transactions were carried out, in the absence of contractual relations, on or after 1 January 2004.

[3] Laws that EU Member States have put in place to give effect to the Second Money Laundering Directive (2001/97/EC) provide a mechanism to identify the owners of companies including companies that have issued bearer shares. The Directive extends the customer identification, recordkeeping and reporting of suspicious transaction requirements which previously applied to credit and financial institutions to a range of professions including auditors, external accountants and tax advisers in the exercise of their professional activities as well as notaries and other independent legal advisers where they assist in the planning or execution of transactions for their clients, concerning among other things the creation, management or operation of trusts, companies or other similar structures. Pursuant to the Third Money Laundering Directive (2005/60/EC), which must be implemented in EU Member States by 15 December 2007, the range of persons covered by customer identification, record keeping and reporting requirements is further extended to include, among others, trust and company service providers. Moreover, customer due diligence requirements are expressly extended to beneficial owners, i.e. the natural persons who ultimately own or control the customer or on whose behalf a transaction or activity is being conducted.

[4] The EU Savings Tax Directive (2003/48/EC) which deals with the taxation of savings income in the form of interest payments seeks to ensure that individuals resident in EU Member States who receive income from another Member State are subject to effective taxation in the Member State in which they are resident for tax purposes. Article 2 of the Directive requires each Member State to adopt and ensure the application of procedures to allow paying agents to establish the identity and residence of their customers (beneficial owners), who are individuals. Paying agents must identify beneficial owners of interest irrespective of whether a debt instrument is in registered or bearer form. During a transitional period domestic and international bonds and other negotiable debt securities first issued before 1 March 2001 will not be regarded as being within the scope of the Directive provided no further issue of those securities was made after 1 March 2002. Additional rules apply if further issues of those securities were made after 1 March 2002. There are different obligations placed on paying agents regarding the procedures to be followed to establish the identity and residence of their customers depending on whether contractual relations were entered into before or after January 2004.

D.   Availability of Ownership, Identity and Accounting Information

Table D.1
Ownership Information-Companies

Table D.1 shows the type of ownership information required to be held by governmental authorities (**column 2**), at the company level (**column 3**) and by service providers, including banks, corporate service providers and other persons (**column 4**).

Explanation of columns 2 through 5

The term "governmental authority" (column 2) includes corporate registries, regulatory authorities, tax authorities and authorities to which publicly traded companies report. Ownership information required to be kept at the company level (column 3) would normally be held in a shareholder register. The requirement on service providers (column 4) managing or providing services to a company to keep identity information typically arises under either specific laws regulating the corporate service provider business or under applicable anti-money laundering laws or under both. Some explanatory comments are provided for some of the countries in **column 5**.

Note that the table makes a distinction between requirements to report or keep legal and beneficial ownership. Legal ownership refers to the registered owner of the share, which may be an individual, but also a nominee, a trust or a company, *etc.* Beneficial ownership reporting requirements refers to a range of reporting requirements that require further information when the legal owner is not also the beneficial owner.

Where a company may issue bearer shares, thereby limiting the requirement to report or keep ownership information, this is mentioned in the table.

Table D.1   Ownership Information Companies

1	2	3	4	5
Country and type of company (if necessary)	**Ownership information required to be held by:**			
	Governmental Authority	**Company**	**Service provider or other person**	**Special rules**
Andorra	Legal and beneficial ownership.	Legal ownership.	External accountants, tax advisors and notaries are required to identify the beneficial owners of companies where they participate in the establishment, management or control of companies. In addition, anti-money laundering legislation requires financial institutions and other service providers to identify the beneficial owners of companies which are their customers and to maintain records of such identification.	Companies generally required to have two thirds Andorran resident owned capital. In any event, Andorran nationals and foreigners allowed to own businesses in Andorra are not permitted to act under fiduciary or nominee arrangements.
Anguilla *Companies incorporated under the Companies Act*	Ultimate beneficial ownership for regulated activities. Legal ownership for other activities.	Legal ownership.	1. Nominees that are licensed service providers – beneficial ownership.* 2. Fiduciary service providers – ultimate beneficial ownership.*	*Does not apply to domestic companies engaged exclusively in domestic activities.
Anguilla *Companies incorporated under the International Business Companies Act*	No*	Legal ownership for other than bearer shares.	1. Nominees that are licensed service providers – beneficial ownership. 2. Fiduciary service providers – ultimate beneficial ownership.	*International Business Companies may not engage in regulated activities.
Anguilla *Limited Liability Companies*	No*	Legal ownership.	1. Nominees that are licensed service providers – beneficial ownership. 2. Fiduciary service providers – ultimate beneficial ownership.	*Limited Liability Companies may not engage in regulated activities.
Antigua and Barbuda *Companies incorporated under the Companies Act*	No	Legal ownership.	No information.	

Table D.1   Ownership Information Companies

1	2	3	4	5
Country and type of company (if necessary)	**Ownership information required to be held by:**			
	Governmental Authority	**Company**	**Service provider or other person**	**Special rules**
Antigua and Barbuda *Companies incorporated under the International Business Companies Act*	No. However, ultimate beneficial ownership information must be reported for regulated activities.	Legal ownership	No information.	
Aruba	No. However, ultimate beneficial ownership information must in most cases be reported to the tax authorities. Companies engaged in regulated activities must report ultimate beneficial ownership information.	Legal ownership for other than bearer shares.	Anti-money laundering due diligence requirements apply to certain service providers.*	*A Bill has been submitted to Parliament obliging corporate service providers to hold information on their clients' ultimate beneficial owners. Pending the enactment of this Bill, corporate service providers that are members of the Aruba Financial Center Association have agreed to voluntarily apply "know your customer" procedures.
Argentina	Legal ownership (changes need not be reported).	Legal ownership.	Anti-money laundering customer due diligence requirements apply to certain service providers.	Financial intermediaries are required to identify their customers on the basis of reliable documents.
Australia	Legal ownership (where applicable, also data on ultimate holding company). Changes of ownership with respect to the largest twenty shareholders must be notified.	Legal ownership (where applicable, also data on ultimate holding company). Listed companies are required to hold and disclose information concerning all "substantial" shareholdings (5% or more), whether legal or beneficial. Non-listed companies must indicate in the register any shares that a member does not hold beneficially.	Nominees that are financial service licensees – beneficial ownership.	- Notices to identify beneficial owners of listed companies can be issued by the regulator and/or the company. - There are no requirements for foreign companies to disclose ownership information. However the tax return must disclose any ultimate parent company. - There are tax reporting requirements identifying all shareholders to whom dividends are paid.
Austria *AG*	No	Legal ownership for other than bearer shares.	See footnote 1.	
Austria *GmbH*	Legal ownership.	Legal ownership.		

Table D.1   Ownership Information Companies

1	2	3	4	5
Country and type of company (if necessary)	**Ownership information required to be held by:**			
	Governmental Authority	**Company**	**Service provider or other person**	**Special rules**
The Bahamas *Companies incorporated under the International Business Companies Act*	None*	Legal ownership.	1. Nominees that are licensed service providers – beneficial ownership. 2. Licensed fiduciary service providers – beneficial ownership. 3. Anti-money laundering legislation requires designated financial institutions to conduct customer due diligence including identification of beneficial owners.	*In the case of public companies that have prospectuses that are registered in The Bahamas, they must also submit information on the ultimate beneficial owner to the Regulator upon request.
The Bahamas *Companies incorporated under the Companies Act*	Legal ownership.*	Legal ownership.*	Anti-money laundering legislation requires designated financial institutions to conduct customer due diligence including identification of beneficial owners.	*In the case of public companies that have prospectuses that are registered in The Bahamas, they must also submit information on the ultimate beneficial owner upon request to the Regulator.
Bahrain	Legal ownership.	Legal ownership.	Under Bahrain's anti-money laundering laws, financial businesses and certain designated non-financial business and professionals are required to undertake proper customer due diligence and maintain adequate customer identification records.	
Barbados	No. However, ultimate beneficial ownership must be reported for regulated activities.	Legal ownership.	Anti-money laundering legislation requires various categories of service providers to perform customer due diligence.	
Belgium	Legal ownership (changes need not be reported). Entities engaged in regulated activities are subject to specific legislative requirements to disclose natural or legal persons that control directly or indirectly holdings exceeding certain thresholds (*e.g.* 5% for credit institutions).	Legal ownership for other than bearer shares.	See footnote 1.	
Belize *Companies Act*	Legal ownership.	Legal ownership.	Legal ownership.	

Table D.1 Ownership Information Companies

1	2	3	4	5
Country and type of company (if necessary)	**Ownership information required to be held by:**			
	Governmental Authority	**Company**	**Service provider or other person**	**Special rules**
Belize *Companies incorporated under the International Business Companies Act*	No. However, IBCs engaged in regulated activities must report ultimate beneficial ownership information.	Legal ownership for other than bearer shares.	1. Licensed service providers – beneficial ownership. 2. Fiduciary service providers – ultimate beneficial ownership.	
Bermuda	Ultimate beneficial ownership (changes need not be reported unless shares are issued to or transferred to a non-resident).	Legal ownership. Beneficial ownership where private companies transfer or issue shares to a non-resident.	Anti- money laundering legislation requires banks, trust companies, deposit companies and regulated businesses to carry out customer due diligence.	
British Virgin Islands *Companies incorporated under the Companies Act*	Legal ownership.*	Legal ownership for all companies other than companies issuing bearer shares.	1. Nominees that are licensed service providers – beneficial ownership 2. Fiduciary service providers – ultimate beneficial ownership.	*Companies engaged in a financial activity requiring a licence from the Financial Services Commission must report to the Financial Services Commission the updated information on the ultimate beneficial owners.
British Virgin Islands *Companies incorporated under the International Business Companies Act and Business Companies Act*	No. However, IBCs engaged in regulated activities must report ultimate beneficial ownership information.			
Brunei *Domestic companies*	No information.	Legal ownership.	No information.	
Brunei *International Business companies*	No	Legal ownership.	Applicable anti- money laundering legislation requires service providers to carry out customer due diligence.*	*IBCs are incorporated by trust companies. With the constituent documents must be filed a Certificate of Due Diligence, which contains an undertaking by the trust company concerned that the IBC complies with applicable provisions and that due diligence in respect of beneficial owners and the source of funding has been conducted, or will be conducted prior to commencement of business. A similar certificate must be filed at each annual renewal.

Table D.1   Ownership Information Companies

1	2	3	4	5
Country and type of company (if necessary)	Ownership information required to be held by:			
	Governmental Authority	Company	Service provider or other person	Special rules
Canada	No*	Legal ownership for other than bearer shares.	Nominees are required to know the next legal owner.	*Where subject to taxation a company may be required to provide ownership information.
Cayman Islands - Ordinary companies - Exempt companies - Non-resident companies	Legal ownership (other than for bearer shares**). Beneficial ownership in relation to: (i) initial subscribers; (ii) members, via annual filing of register of members (except for exempted companies).	Legal and beneficial ownership (other than for bearer shares**)-all companies (including exempted companies, although later not required to file same) must keep a register of members.	All persons providing company services* are regulated by CIMA and such services are defined as "relevant financial business" under anti-money laundering / counter financing of terrorism regime, and therefore service providers must apply know your customer and recordkeeping requirements.	*e.g. nominees; bearer share custodians; directors/officers; formation services. **Bearer shares are required to be immobilised and the beneficial ownership details held by the authorised or recognised custodian.
China	Legal ownership.	Legal ownership for other than bearer shares.*	N/A	*Bearer shares have never been issued in practice.
Cook Islands *Companies incorporated under the Companies Act*	Legal ownership.	Legal ownership.	Anti-money laundering legislation requires service providers to carry out due diligence where applicable.	
Cook Islands *Companies incorporated under the International Companies Act*	No. However, companies engaged in regulated activities must report ultimate beneficial ownership information.	Legal ownership for other than bearer shares*.	Trust and company service providers (trustee companies) are included in the definition of "financial institution" under anti-money laundering legislation. and must therefore identify their customers including, in the case of legal entities, their principal owners and beneficiaries	*Bearer shares must be held by an approved custodian.
Costa Rica	Beneficial ownership.	Beneficial ownership.	Applicable anti- money laundering legislation requires financial institutions to carry out customer due diligence.	
Cyprus	Legal ownership (changes need not be reported). Foreign banks and International Collective Investment Schemes are required to disclose ultimate beneficial ownership, unless the company is beneficially owned by EU nationals.	Legal ownership.	See footnote 1.	

Table D.1 Ownership Information Companies

1	2	3	4	5
Country and type of company (if necessary)	Ownership information required to be held by:			
	Governmental Authority	Company	Service provider or other person	Special rules
Czech Republic	Legal ownership.*	Legal ownership.*	See footnote 1.	*Ownership information on bearer shares may not be available in some cases.
Denmark	No. However, for taxation purposes a company is required to provide information on owners who own more than 25% of the capital or control 50% or more of the voting rights. Banks and other regulated companies are required to report the names of owners with a direct or indirect shareholding of at least 10% of either the capital or the votes or a shareholding that otherwise gives considerable influence upon the management of the company.	Legal ownership other than for bearer shares. Also, any person who controls more than 5 % of the votes or the capital of a Public Limited Company shall inform the company of the said shareholding. The company must record this major shareholding in a register which is open for public inspection.	See footnote 1.	
Dominica *Companies incorporated under the Companies Act*	No*	Legal ownership.	No information.	*Companies incorporated under the Companies Act may not engage in regulated activities.
Dominica *Companies incorporated under the International Business Company Act*	No. However, companies engaged in regulated activities must report ultimate beneficial ownership information.	Legal ownership other than for bearer shares.	1. Nominees that are licensed service providers – beneficial ownership. 2. Fiduciary service providers – ultimate beneficial ownership.	
Finland	No	Legal ownership.	See footnote 1.	
France - *Public limited liability company* - *Limited partnerships with share capital* - *Simplified joint-stock companies*	Legal ownership (changes need not be reported).	Legal ownership other than for bearer shares.*	Registered intermediaries holding securities on behalf of third parties are subject to procedures that make it possible to identify these owners. See also footnote 1.	*Information on bearer securities may be obtained from the central repository of financial instruments.
France *Private limited liability company*	Legal ownership.	Legal ownership.	See footnote 1.	

Table D.1   Ownership Information Companies

1	2	3	4	5
Country and type of company (if necessary)	**Ownership information required to be held by:**			
	Governmental Authority	**Company**	**Service provider or other person**	**Special rules**
France - *Partnerships* - *Limited liability partnerships*	Legal ownership (except for limited partners).	Legal ownership.	See footnote 1.	
Germany *AG and KGaA*	Legal ownership (changes need not be reported). Legal ownership information must be reported where shareholder in a listed AG exceeds 5, 10, 25, 50 or 75 % of voting rights (direct control and attribution of indirect control). Legal ownership information must be reported where shareholder in an unlisted AG owns more than 25 or 50% of shares (direct control and attribution of indirect control).	Legal ownership other than for bearer shares. Legal ownership information must always be reported where shareholder in a listed AG exceeds 5, 10, 25, 50 or 75 % of voting rights (direct control and attribution of indirect control). Legal ownership information must always be reported where shareholder in an unlisted AG owns more than 25 or 50% of shares (direct control and attribution of indirect control).	Notaries and other service providers involved in the incorporation process - beneficial ownership. For subsequent shareholders, see footnote 1.	
Germany *GmbH*	Legal ownership.	Legal ownership.	Notaries and other service providers involved in the incorporation process - beneficial ownership. Any change in shareholder composition requires a notarial deed and notaries are covered by anti-money laundering obligations. See footnote 1.	*German company law does not contain the distinction between legal and beneficial owners of shares. There are only ordinary shareholders. A shareholder acting as an undisclosed agent for a third party has the same rights and obligations as every other shareholder (and is subject to tax on any profit distributions). Where an intermediary acts as a disclosed agent, the third party and not the intermediary is identified as the shareholder.
Gibraltar	Legal ownership.	Legal ownership.	1. Nominees that are licensed service providers – beneficial ownership. 2. Fiduciary service providers – ultimate beneficial ownership.	
Greece	No information.	No information.	See footnote 1.	
Grenada *Companies incorporated under the Companies Act*	No information.	No information.	No information.	

Table D.1   Ownership Information Companies

1	2	3	4	5
Country and type of company (if necessary)	Ownership information required to be held by:			
	Governmental Authority	**Company**	**Service provider or other person**	**Special rules**
Grenada *Companies incorporated under the International Companies Act*	No. However, companies engaged in a regulated activity requiring a licence must report updated information on the ultimate beneficial owners.	Legal ownership for other than bearer shares.	1. Nominees that are licensed service providers – beneficial ownership. 2. Fiduciary service providers – ultimate beneficial ownership.	
Guatemala	No	Legal ownership for other than bearer shares.	No	
Guernsey	Beneficial ownership.*	Legal ownership and beneficial ownership.	Trust and company service providers are required to be licensed and to know the beneficial owners of companies to which they provide services pursuant to anti-money laundering rules.	*Beneficial ownership of all companies must be provided to the authorities before incorporation. Changes in the beneficial owners of exempt and international companies must be notified to the authorities.
Hong Kong, China	Legal ownership (annual return). Anyone with an interest (including a beneficial interest) of 5% or more of the voting shares of a listed corporation (including companies and other types of body corporates) is required to disclose that interest within 3 business days after the day on which the acquisition or disposal of the interest occurred. Further movements which take their interests through a whole percentage level (*e.g.* 6%, 7%) must also be disclosed.	Legal ownership.	Financial institutions, such as banking, securities and insurance institutions are required under enforceable anti-money laundering guidelines to conduct customer due diligence and keep such record, including the record of beneficial owners.*	*Hong Kong, China intends to draft legislation to implement fully the legislative requirements under FATF Recommendation 5 (customer due diligence) among others after the FATF Mutual Evaluation is completed in June 2008.
Hungary *(Limited and unlimited partnerships are also covered by this table)*	Legal ownership except for public companies.*	Legal ownership (including disclosure of nominee shareholdings).	Lawyer/notary on registration of a new company must verify the identities of all founding shareholders. See also footnote 1.	*If the shareholder/member is a foreign legal person or foreign natural person without a Hungarian registered office/residential address a "delivery agent" must be specified.
Iceland	No. However, all public limited companies are obliged to register their shares with Icelandic Securities Depositary Ltd.	Legal ownership.	Anti-money laundering know your customer requirements apply to certain service providers.	

Table D.1   Ownership Information Companies

1	2	3	4	5
Country and type of company (if necessary)	Ownership information required to be held by:			
	Governmental Authority	Company	Service provider or other person	Special rules
Ireland *Private limited company*	Legal ownership. Irish incorporated non-resident companies must notify Revenue Commissioners of beneficial owners.	Legal ownership.*	See footnote 1.	*Directors/secretaries required to notify the company of shares in which they or their families have an interest. This information should be maintained in a separate register.
Ireland *Public limited company*	Legal ownership.	Legal ownership other than for bearer shares.*	See footnote 1.	*Company must be notified by any person or group acquiring or disposing of any form of interest that brings their shareholding above or below 5%. This information is required to be maintained in a separate register.
Ireland *Investment company*	No	Beneficial ownership.*	See footnote 1.*	*Investment companies and their managers are designated bodies for anti-money laundering purposes.
Isle of Man	Legal ownership. Companies engaged in regulated activities must provide details of their ultimate beneficial owner.	Legal ownership.	Corporate service providers must ensure they retain a copy of all nominee agreements or other such trust instruments. Anti-money laundering legislation requires corporate service providers to know the beneficial owner of any company to which they provide services. Companies incorporated under the new Companies Act 2006 are required at all times to have a registered agent in the Isle of Man. A registered agent must hold a licence under the Fiduciary Services Acts and is responsible for maintaining various records and information including details of legal and beneficial ownership.	
Italy	Legal ownership.	Legal ownership for other than bearer shares.	See footnote 1.	

Table D.1   Ownership Information Companies

1	2	3	4	5
Country and type of company (if necessary)	Ownership information required to be held by:			
	Governmental Authority	Company	Service provider or other person	Special rules
Japan - *Limited and unlimited partnerships* - *Limited liability companies* - *Joint stock companies*	Legal ownership (joint stock companies need not report changes).	Legal ownership and beneficial ownership.	Anti-money laundering legislation requires financial service providers to undertake customer due diligence.	
Jersey	All companies must report ultimate beneficial ownership to the Financial Services Commission (local companies need not report subsequent changes in ownership). All companies must report legal ownership to the Register of Companies. Entities engaged in regulated activities must report ultimate beneficial ownership information to the Financial Services Commission.	Legal ownership and beneficial ownership.	Trust and company service providers are required to be licensed and to know the beneficial owners of companies to which they provide services pursuant to anti-money laundering rules.	Changes in the beneficial owners of exempt and international business companies must be notified to the authorities.
Korea - *Unlimited Partnership Company* - *Limited Partnership Company* - *Joint-Stock Company* - *Limited liability company*	Legal ownership.	Legal ownership.	Anti-money laundering legislation requires financial service providers to undertake customer due diligence.	

Table D.1   Ownership Information Companies

1	2	3	4	5
Country and type of company (if necessary)	Ownership information required to be held by:			
	Governmental Authority	Company	Service provider or other person	Special rules
Liechtenstein *AG*	No*	Yes**	**Liechtenstein anti-money laundering rules require that at least one person acting as an organ or director of a legal entity that does not conduct any commercial business in its country of domicile is obliged to identify and record the ultimate beneficial owner. Other service providers covered by anti-money laundering rules may also hold ownership information where they engage in relevant business contact with the company (*e.g.* a bank opening an account for the company).	*Special ownership disclosure requirements apply to banks, finance companies, investment undertakings, insurance companies and major holdings in publicly traded companies.
Liechtenstein *GmbH*	Legal ownership for all shareholders.*	Yes**		
Liechtenstein *K-AG*	Legal ownership for shareholders with unlimited liability.*	Yes**		
Luxembourg *Companies limited by shares*	Legal ownership* (changes need not be reported).*	Legal ownership.**	See footnote 1.	*Tax reporting requirements may apply. **If the legal owner is not the beneficial owner, the latter has to be disclosed to the tax authorities.
Luxembourg *Limited Liability Company*	Legal ownership.	Legal ownership.	See footnote 1.	
Macao, China - *General partnerships* - *Limited partnerships* - *Private companies* - *Public companies*	Legal ownership.	Legal ownership for other than bearer shares.	Anti-money laundering customer due diligence requirements apply to financial institutions.	
Malaysia	Legal ownership.*	Legal ownership.	The anti-money laundering legislation requires virtually all persons managing or providing financial services to a company to perform customer due diligence.	*No ownership information is required to be kept for Labuan companies other than those engaged in a regulated activity who must report the names and addresses of shareholders holding 10% or more of the voting shares.
Malta	Legal ownership.	Legal ownership.	See footnote 1.	

Table D.1 Ownership Information Companies

1	2	3	4	5
Country and type of company (if necessary)	Ownership information required to be held by:			
	Governmental Authority	Company	Service provider or other person	Special rules
Marshall Islands *Corporations*	Legal ownership (changes need not be reported). Beneficial ownership if a majority of the corporations in a corporate program either directly hold a vessel or indirectly relate to its maritime programme. Financial institutions are required to file an annual ownership control report form.	Legal ownership for other than bearer shares.	Anti-money laundering know your customer requirements apply to cash dealers and financial institutions.*	*The Marshall Islands requires that the request to form a corporation / limited liability company is made by a qualified intermediary (*i.e.* attorney or accountant). The intermediary is expected to conduct due diligence and certify that the corporation / company will not be used for illegal purposes. If the Registry is uncomfortable with the intermediary, it may refuse to form the corporation / company or require the name(s) of the beneficial owner(s).
Marshall Islands *Limited Liability Companies*	No	Legal ownership.		
Mauritius *Local companies*	Legal ownership.	Legal ownership.		
Mauritius *Category 1 Global Business Companies*	Legal and beneficial ownership.	Legal and beneficial ownership.	Legal and beneficial ownership.	
Mauritius *Category 2 Global Business Companies*	No*	Legal and beneficial ownership.	Legal and beneficial ownership.	*However, information on beneficial ownership should be provided upon request to regulatory authorities.
Mexico	Legal ownership.	Legal ownership.	Anti-money laundering legislation requires financial service providers to undertake customer due diligence.	
Monaco - *General partnership* - *Limited partnership* - *Public company* - *Limited partnership with share capital*	Legal (beneficial) ownership.*	Legal ownership (legal ownership for public companies for other than bearer shares).	Anti-money laundering due diligence requirements apply.	*Under Monegasque law only legal ownership is recognised, the distinction between "beneficial owner" and "legal owner" being unknown. As a result, the identity of partners in a partnership and of shareholders in a joint stock company is that of the actual owners. The nominee concept is not recognised by Monegasque law.

Table D.1   Ownership Information Companies

1	2	3	4	5
Country and type of company (if necessary)	**Ownership information required to be held by:**			
	Governmental Authority	**Company**	**Service provider or other person**	**Special rules**
Montserrat *Companies incorporated under the Companies Act*	No. However, companies engaged in a regulated activity requiring a licence must report updated information on the ultimate beneficial owners.	Legal ownership.	1. Nominees that are licensed service providers – legal and beneficial owner. 2. Fiduciary service providers – ultimate beneficial owner.	
Montserrat *Companies incorporated under the International Business Companies Act*	No*	Legal ownership for other than bearer shares.	1. Nominees that are licensed service providers – legal and beneficial owner. 2. Fiduciary service providers – ultimate beneficial owner.	*IBCs may not carry out regulated activities.
Montserrat *Companies incorporated under the Limited Liability Company Act*	No*	No	1. Nominees that are licensed service providers – legal and beneficial owner. 2. Fiduciary service providers – ultimate beneficial owner.	*LLCs may not carry out regulated activities.
Nauru	Legal ownership (ownership information need not be provided in some defined cases).	Legal ownership for other than bearer shares.	Financial institutions including trust and company service providers are required to verify their customers' identity.	
Netherlands	Legal ownership (changes need not be reported unless the company is 100% owned).	Listed companies: Shares are traded at the stock exchange through an intermediary (bank) which registers the shareholders. Shareholders must inform the company and a supervisory authority when they acquire 5 % or more of the shares. Unlisted companies: Legal ownership for other than bearer shares.	See footnote 1.	
Netherlands Antilles	No. However, companies engaged in banking and other regulated activities must report ultimate beneficial ownership information. Ultimate beneficial ownership information must in most cases be reported to the tax authorities.	Legal ownership for other than bearer shares.	Service providers are required to establish ultimate beneficial ownership.	

Table D.1   Ownership Information Companies

1	2	3	4	5
Country and type of company (if necessary)	Ownership information required to be held by:			
	Governmental Authority	Company	Service provider or other person	Special rules
New Zealand	Legal ownership.	Legal ownership.	Nominees are required to know the next legal owner and are required to lodge an annual return to the Companies Office in respect of the person on whose behalf securities are registered in their name. Anti-money laundering know your customer requirements apply to certain service providers.	
Niue *Domestic companies*	Legal ownership.	Legal ownership.	Pursuant to the Financial Transactions Report Act, financial institutions are required to verify their customers' identity.	
Niue *International Business Companies*	No, however, companies engaged in a financial activity requiring a licence must report updated information on the ultimate beneficial owners.	Legal ownership for other than bearer shares.	Pursuant to the Financial Transactions Report Act, financial institutions are required to verify their customers' identity.	
Norway	Legal ownership for public companies.	Legal ownership.	Anti-money laundering legislation requires financial service providers to undertake customer due diligence.	
Panama - *Joint-stock corporations* - *Limited liability companies* - *General partnership* - *Limited partnership* - *Partnership limited by shares*	- Legal ownership (changes to shareholders of joint-stock corporations need not be reported). Beneficial ownership of controlling shareholders of publicly traded companies. Companies carrying on regulated activities must provide details of their beneficial owners.	- Legal ownership for other than bearer shares. Beneficial ownership of controlling shareholders of publicly traded companies.	Banks, trust companies, exchange and settlement houses, financial institutions, savings and loan co-operatives, stock exchanges, stockbrokers, dealers in securities and investment managers and other service providers are obliged to adequately identify their clients. A lawyer acting as resident agent of a joint-stock corporation is required to "know its client".	

Table D.1   Ownership Information Companies

1	2	3	4	5
Country and type of company (if necessary)	**Ownership information required to be held by:**			
	Governmental Authority	**Company**	**Service provider or other person**	**Special rules**
Philippines	Legal ownership (stock corporations need not report changes unless such obligations arise under separate investment incentive laws). Companies carrying on regulated activities must provide details of their beneficial owners.	Legal ownership.	The Anti-Money Laundering Act requires financial institutions to undertake customer due diligence.	
Poland	No	Legal ownership.	See footnote 1.	
Portugal *Trading companies (which includes all types of partnerships)*	Legal ownership. Shareholders/members who are members of the Board of Directors must be identified (tax law requirement).	Legal ownership. For bearer shares please see Table C3.	See footnote 1.	
Portugal *Joint-stock companies*	No. Shareholders who are members of the Board of Directors must be identified (tax law requirement).	Legal ownership other than for bearer shares.	See footnote 1.	
Russian Federation	Legal ownership.	Legal ownership.	Anti-money laundering legislation requires legal and accounting service providers to carry out customer due diligence.	
Saint Kitts and Nevis (Saint Kitts) *Companies incorporated under the Companies Act Ordinary companies*	Legal ownership. Companies engaged in a regulated activity requiring a licence must report updated information on the ultimate beneficial owners.	Legal ownership.	1. Nominees that are licensed service providers – legal and beneficial owner. 2. Fiduciary service providers – ultimate beneficial owner.	
Saint Kitts and Nevis (Saint Kitts) *Companies incorporated under the Companies Act Exempt companies*	No. However, companies engaged in a regulated activity requiring a licence must report updated information on the ultimate beneficial owners.	Legal ownership for other than bearer shares.	1. Nominees that are licensed service providers – legal and beneficial owner. 2. Fiduciary service providers – ultimate beneficial owner.	

Table D.1 Ownership Information Companies

1	2	3	4	5
Country and type of company (if necessary)	**Ownership information required to be held by:**			
	Governmental Authority	**Company**	**Service provider or other person**	**Special rules**
Saint Kitts and Nevis (Nevis) *Companies incorporated under the Limited Liability Company Ordinance*	No. However, limited liability companies engaged in a regulated activity requiring a licence must report information on the ultimate beneficial owners.	No	1. Nominees that are licensed service providers – legal and beneficial owner. 2. Fiduciary service providers – ultimate beneficial owner.	
Saint Kitts and Nevis (Nevis) *Companies incorporated under the Nevis Business Corporation Ordinance*	No. However, corporations engaged in a regulated activity requiring a licence must report information on the ultimate beneficial owners.	Legal ownership for other than bearer shares.	1. Nominees that are licensed service providers – legal and beneficial owner. 2. Fiduciary service providers – ultimate beneficial owner.	
Saint Lucia *Companies incorporated under the Companies Act*	Legal ownership.*	Legal ownership.	Anti-money laundering know your customer requirements apply to persons providing financial services.	*Companies incorporated under the Companies Act may only do business in the local sector.
Saint Lucia *Companies incorporated under the International Business Companies Act*	No. However, companies engaged in a regulated activity requiring a licence must report updated information on the ultimate beneficial owners.	Legal ownership.	1. Nominees that are licensed service providers – legal and beneficial owner. 2. Fiduciary service providers – ultimate beneficial owner.	
Saint Vincent and the Grenadines *Companies incorporated under the Companies Act ("domestic companies")*	Legal ownership.*	Legal ownership.	Anti-money laundering laws require financial institutions, which include designated non-financial businesses and certain professionals, to undertake proper customer due diligence and maintain adequate customer identification records. These laws apply to both the domestic and the international financial sector.	*Companies incorporated under the Companies Act may only do business in the local sector.

Table D.1 Ownership Information Companies

1	2	3	4	5
Country and type of company (if necessary)	**Ownership information required to be held by:**			
	Governmental Authority	**Company**	**Service provider or other person**	**Special rules**
Saint Vincent and the Grenadines *Companies incorporated under the International Business Companies Act*	No. However, companies engaged in a regulated activity requiring a licence must disclose ab initio as well as report updated information on the ultimate beneficial owners.	Legal ownership for other than bearer shares.	Service provider or licensed agents and trustees or financial fiduciaries are required to know all relevant legal and ultimate beneficial ownership information on their clients.	
Samoa *Domestic companies*	Legal ownership. Companies engaged in regulated activities must provide information on ultimate beneficial owners.	Legal ownership.	Anti-money laundering know your customer requirements apply to certain service providers.	
Samoa *International companies*	International companies – Legal ownership (changes need not be reported). Segregated Funds International Companies – Legal ownership (changes need not be reported). Shareless or Creditor controlled international companies - No (control of the company is exercised by use of a bearer debenture). International companies engaged in regulated activities must provide information on ultimate beneficial owners.*	Legal ownership other than for bearer shares. Segregated Funds International Companies and other companies engaged in regulated activities may not issue bearer shares.	Anti-money laundering know your customer requirements apply to certain service providers. All documents required by the Registrar of International and Foreign Companies must be lodged or filed by or through a licensed trustee company. Such companies (but not partnerships) are required by the anti-money laundering rules to identify the beneficial owners of corporate clients.	
San Marino *Private limited liability company/stock corporation*	Legal ownership.	Legal ownership for other than bearer shares.	Anti-money laundering know your customer requirements apply to certain credit and financial institutions. In the context of companies, the obligation to identify customers means that certified copies of the articles of association, of industry and commerce licenses, certification of persons representing the company, power to sign and proxies by the General Meeting or the Board of Directors must be supplied.	

Table D.1   Ownership Information Companies

1	2	3	4	5
Country and type of company (if necessary)	Ownership information required to be held by:			
	Governmental Authority	Company	Service provider or other person	Special rules
San Marino *Anonymous stock corporation*	Legal ownership (changes need not be reported).* Banks and non-bank financial institutions must provide information on ultimate beneficial owners as part of the licensing process. The identity of owners acquiring 5% or more of the shares must be reported.	Legal ownership for other than bearer shares. Under the law n° 130 which entered into force 11 December 2006 as from January 1 2008, the anonymous stock corporations' meetings must be held in presence of a notary public who has to identify the holder of bearer shares and keep the identity information for 5 years. Such information can be obtained only from judicial authority.	Anti-money laundering know your customer requirements apply to certain credit and financial institutions. In the context of companies, the obligation to identify customers means that certified copies of the articles of association, of industry and commerce licenses, certification of persons representing the company, power to sign and proxies by the General Meeting or the Board of Directors must be supplied.	*All capital subscribers are known upon incorporation. When the capital stock has been paid up, then it can be made up of bearer shares, even for the whole amount.
Seychelles *Companies incorporated under the Companies Act (includes Protected Cell Companies and Special Purpose companies)*	Legal ownership.	Legal ownership for other than bearer shares.*	Anti-money laundering know your customer requirements apply to persons providing financial services.**	*Legislative amendment under way to prohibit the issuance of bearer shares. **Anti-money laundering legislation being revised to require corporate service providers (including those acting as nominees) to identify the ultimate beneficial owners.
Seychelles *Companies incorporated under the International Business Companies Act*	Legal ownership.	Legal ownership for other than bearer shares.*	Legislative amendments to the International Business Companies Act 1994 requires identification of the owners of bearer shares to be held by the service provider in Seychelles or in the office of another intermediary or agent in another jurisdiction.**	*Legislative amendment under way to require company directors to know the ultimate beneficial owners of issued bearer shares. **Anti-money laundering legislation being revised to require corporate service providers (including those acting as nominees) to identify the ultimate beneficial owners.
Singapore	Legal ownership.	Legal ownership. In addition, public listed companies are required to keep a register of "substantial shareholders" (i.e. persons having legal, beneficial or deemed interests in 5% or more of voting shares).	Legal and Beneficial ownership. Anti-money laundering and counter financing of terrorism (AML/CFT) legislation and guidelines require persons providing financial, legal and accounting services to conduct customer due diligence.	

Table D.1   Ownership Information Companies

1	2	3	4	5
Country and type of company (if necessary)	Ownership information required to be held by:			
	Governmental Authority	Company	Service provider or other person	Special rules
Slovak Republic - *General partnership* - *Limited partnership* - *Limited liability company*	Legal ownership.*	Legal ownership.**	See footnote 1.	*The legal ownership reporting requirement applies to public limited liability company only if it has a sole shareholder. **Legal ownership for other than bearer shares for public limited liability companies.
South Africa	Legal ownership (changes need not be reported).	Legal ownership.	Nominees must disclose beneficial ownership to the issuing company. Anti-money laundering legislation requires service providers to conduct customer due diligence.	
Spain	Legal ownership. Shareholdings in credit institutions of more than 5% must be disclosed and registered.	Legal ownership for other than bearer shares.	See footnote 1.	
Sweden	No. However, banks, financial institutions and insurance companies must provide beneficial ownership information to regulatory authorities.*	Legal ownership.	See footnote 1.	*Sweden keeps information in a wide range of registers and the documentation in some cases contains information about companies' owners.
Switzerland *Company limited by shares*	Legal ownership (changes need not be reported).*	Legal ownership for other than bearer shares (unless the bearer share holder is a founding shareholder).*	Pursuant to Swiss anti-money laundering law, the organs, resident in Switzerland, of domiciliary companies are considered to be financial intermediaries and are therefore under the obligation to identify the beneficial owners. In other cases (*i.e.* companies other than domiciliary companies) anti-money laundering law may still require service providers to identify and record beneficial ownership (*i.e.* Swiss bank opens a bank account for a company).	*In connection with companies listed on a Swiss stock exchange, any holding of voting rights of 5% or more must be disclosed to the company and the stock exchange.
Switzerland *Limited liability company*	Legal ownership.*	Legal ownership.*		

Table D.1 Ownership Information Companies

1	2	3	4	5
Country and type of company (if necessary)	**Ownership information required to be held by:**			
	Governmental Authority	**Company**	**Service provider or other person**	**Special rules**
Turkey	Legal ownership. Companies engaged in financial activities and in the electricity market are required to disclose information about ultimate owners.	No (except for banks and other capital market institutions and publicly held companies).	Independent accountants and sworn-in financial advisors must perform customer due diligence.	
Turks and Caicos Islands	No. However, companies engaged in a financial activity requiring a licence from the Financial Services Commission must report updated information on the ultimate beneficial owners.	Legal ownership for other than bearer shares.	1. Nominees that are licensed service providers – legal and beneficial owner. 2. Fiduciary service providers – ultimate beneficial owner.	
United Arab Emirates	Legal ownership. Federal companies that carry on financial activities and all DIFC companies are required to report the names of owners with a direct or indirect shareholding of at least 10% of the shares in the company.	Legal ownership.	Anti-money laundering legislation requires financial service providers to carry out customer due diligence.	
United Kingdom	Legal ownership for private limited companies (annual return).	Legal ownership for private limited companies. Legal ownership other than for bearer shares for public limited companies. A special register of interests in shares must be maintained by public limited companies. The obligation to disclose such interests is on the person holding the interest. The trigger for disclosure is the holding of voting shares which (a) are material and represent >3% of the companies share capital or (b) represent 10% of such share capital.	See footnote 1.	

Table D.1   Ownership Information Companies

1	2	3	4	5
Country and type of company (if necessary)	**Ownership information required to be held by:**			
	Governmental Authority	**Company**	**Service provider or other person**	**Special rules**
United States	Legal ownership information must be provided to the federal government on information returns filed by domestic corporations that pay dividends of more than USD10 in a given year and by domestic corporations that are more than 25 percent foreign owned.	Legal ownership other than for bearer shares.	Anti-money laundering due diligence requirements apply.	Federal tax law imposes special record-keeping requirements on 25 percent foreign owned corporations potentially involved in conduit-financing transactions and requires filing of ownership information in the case of certain transactions with tax avoidance potential. Other potentially applicable laws, such as federal securities laws, may require the filing of ownership information, *e.g.* where ownership of a public corporation exceeds 5 percent.
United States Virgin Islands *Domestic stock corporations*	No	Legal ownership.	No information.	In the case of any company that does business in the USVI, a business license is required to be obtained from the Department of Licensing and Consumer Affairs ("DCLA"). The application for such a license generally requires disclosure of the principals of the business and/or the persons responsible for the business operations in the USVI. Banks and insurance companies are also required to disclose their ownership as part of a licensing process.
United States Virgin Islands *Limited Liability Companies*	No	No	No information.	In the case of any company that does business in the USVI, a business license is required to be obtained from the Department of Licensing and Consumer Affairs ("DCLA"). The application for such a license generally requires disclosure of the principals of the business and/or the persons responsible for the business operations in the USVI. Banks and insurance companies are also required to disclose their ownership as part of a licensing process.

Table D.1   Ownership Information Companies

1	2	3	4	5
Country and type of company (if necessary)	**Ownership information required to be held by:**			
	Governmental Authority	**Company**	**Service provider or other person**	**Special rules**
United States Virgin Islands *Foreign Sales Corporations*	No	Legal ownership.	No information.	In the case of any company that does business in the USVI, a business license is required to be obtained from the Department of Licensing and Consumer Affairs ("DCLA"). The application for such a license generally requires disclosure of the principals of the business and/or the persons responsible for the business operations in the USVI. Banks and insurance companies are also required to disclose their ownership as part of a licensing process.
United States Virgin Islands *Exempt companies*	No	Legal ownership.	No information.	The identity of the shareholders of USVI companies need not be revealed except in response to a proper request from the United States or the USVI tax authorities. In the case of any company that does business in the USVI, a business license is required to be obtained from the Department of Licensing and Consumer Affairs ("DCLA"). The application for such a license generally requires disclosure of the principals of the business and/or the persons responsible for the business operations in the USVI. Banks and insurance companies are also required to disclose their ownership as part of a licensing process.
Uruguay *Joint stock corporation (SA)*	Legal ownership (changes need not be reported). Banks, communication and transportation companies must register details of legal and ultimate owners with regulatory authorities.	Legal ownership.	Service providers covered by anti-money laundering rules may hold ownership information where they engage in relevant business contact with a company.	
Uruguay *SRL*	Legal ownership.	Yes	Anti-money laundering know your customer requirements apply to financial institutions and to managers of commercial companies (other than group companies) where such managers act on behalf and on account of third parties.	

Table D.1   Ownership Information Companies

1	2	3	4	5
Country and type of company (if necessary)	Ownership information required to be held by:			
	Governmental Authority	Company	Service provider or other person	Special rules
Vanuatu *Local companies*	Legal ownership. Beneficial owners of domestic banks must be identified and any change in ownership that results in a person acquiring or exercising power over 20 percent or more of the voting power of the bank must be approved by the relevant regulator.	Legal ownership.	Anti-money laundering know your customer requirements apply to financial institutions and lawyers and accountants to the extent that they receive funds in the course of their business for the purpose of deposit or investment.	
Vanuatu *Exempt companies*	Legal ownership.* (founding beneficial owners). Exempt companies carrying on international banking are required to disclose beneficial ownership and significant changes of ownership must obtain prior approval.	Legal ownership.		*Exempt companies are required to include in their annual return the name, address and nationality of every person for whom, during the period covered by the return, any member has acted as agent or nominee. The requirement does not apply to companies that are not engaged in banking, insurance or trust company business.
Vanuatu *International companies*	Legal ownership (changes need not be reported).	Legal ownership.		

[1] Laws that EU Member States have put in place to give effect to the Second Money Laundering Directive (2001/97/EC) provide a mechanism to identify the owners of companies including companies that have issued bearer shares. The Directive extends the customer identification, recordkeeping and reporting of suspicious transaction requirements which previously applied to credit and financial institutions to a range of professions including auditors, external accountants and tax advisers in the exercise of their professional activities as well as notaries and other independent legal advisers where they assist in the planning or execution of transactions for their clients, concerning among other things the creation, management or operation of trusts, companies or other similar structures. Pursuant to the Third Money Laundering Directive (2005/60/EC), which must be implemented in EU Member States by 15 December 2007, the range of persons covered by customer identification, record keeping and reporting requirements is further extended to include, among others, trust and company service providers. Moreover, customer due diligence requirements are expressly extended to beneficial owners, i.e. the natural persons who ultimately own or control the customer or on whose behalf a transaction or activity is being conducted.

Table D.2
Trusts Laws

Explanation of columns 2 through 4

Column 2 lists the countries that have domestic trust laws and **column 3** lists those countries that have separate domestic trust laws that apply only to non-resident settlors and beneficiaries. **Column 4** lists the countries without trust laws that allow their residents to act as trustees of foreign trusts.

Table D.2   Trusts Laws

1	2	3	4
Country	Domestic trust law	Special laws governing the formation of trusts with non-resident settlors or beneficiaries	Residents can administer foreign law trust (to be completed only by countries without domestic trust law)
Andorra	No	N/A	No
Anguilla	Yes	No	N/A
Antigua and Barbuda	Yes	No information.	N/A
Aruba	No	N/A	No
Argentina	Yes	No	N/a
Australia	Yes	No	N/A
Austria	No	N/A	Yes
The Bahamas	Yes	No	N/A
Bahrain	Yes	No	N/A
Barbados	Yes	Yes	N/A
Belgium	No (however, special provisions recognise and regulate certain aspects of trusts)	N/A	Yes
Belize	Yes	No	N/A
Bermuda	Yes	No	N/A
British Virgin Islands	Yes	No	N/A
Brunei	Yes	Yes	N/A
Canada	Yes	No	N/A
Cayman Islands	Yes	No	N/A
China	Yes	No	N/A
Cook Islands	Yes	Yes	N/A
Costa Rica	Yes	No	N/A
Cyprus	Yes	Yes	N/A
Czech Republic	No	N/A	Yes
Denmark	No	N/A	Yes
Dominica	Yes	Yes	N/A
Finland	No	N/A	Yes
France	No	N/A	No
Germany	No	N/A	Yes
Gibraltar	Yes	No	N/A
Greece	No	N/A	Yes
Grenada	Yes	Yes	N/A
Guatemala	Yes	No	N/A
Guernsey	Yes	No	N/A

Table D.2   Trusts Laws

1	2	3	4
Country	Domestic trust law	Special laws governing the formation of trusts with non-resident settlors or beneficiaries	Residents can administer foreign law trust (to be completed only by countries without domestic trust law)
Hong Kong, China	Yes	No	N/A
Hungary	No	N/A	Yes
Iceland	No	N/A	No
Ireland	Yes	No	N/A
Isle of Man	Yes	No	N/A
Italy	No	N/A	Yes
Japan	Yes	No	N/A
Jersey	Yes	No	N/A
Korea	Yes	No	N/A
Liechtenstein	Yes	No	N/A
Luxembourg	No	N/A	Yes
Macao, China	No	Yes	Yes
Malaysia	Yes	Yes	N/A
Malta	Yes	No	N/A
Marshall Islands	No	N/A	No
Mauritius	Yes	No	N/A
Mexico	Yes	No	N/A
Monaco	No (however special provisions recognise trusts formed under "Anglo-Saxon law")	N/A	Yes
Montserrat	Yes	No	N/A
Nauru	Yes	Yes	N/A
Netherlands	No	N/A	Yes
Netherlands Antilles	No	N/A	Yes
New Zealand	Yes	No	N/A
Niue	Yes	No	N/A
Norway	No	N/A	Yes
Panama	Yes	No	N/A
Philippines	Yes	No	N/A
Poland	No	N/A	No information.
Portugal	No	N/A	Yes
Russian Federation	No	N/A	Yes
Saint Kitts and Nevis	Yes	Yes (Nevis)	N/A
Saint Lucia	Yes	Yes	N/A
Saint Vincent and the Grenadines	Yes	Yes	N/A

Table D.2   Trusts Laws

1	2	3	4
Country	Domestic trust law	Special laws governing the formation of trusts with non-resident settlors or beneficiaries	Residents can administer foreign law trust (to be completed only by countries without domestic trust law)
Samoa	Yes	Yes	N/A
San Marino	Yes	No	N/A
Seychelles	No	Yes	Yes
Singapore	Yes	No	N/A
Slovak Republic	No	N/A	No information.
South Africa	Yes	Yes (exchange control restrictions)	N/A
Spain	No	N/A	No
Sweden	No	N/A	Yes
Switzerland	No	N/A	Yes
Turkey	No	N/A	No information.
Turks and Caicos Islands	Yes	Yes	N/A
United Arab Emirates	Yes	No	N/A
United Kingdom	Yes	No	N/A
United States	Yes	No	N/A
United States Virgin Islands	Yes (United States)	No	N/A
Uruguay	Yes	No	N/A
Vanuatu	Yes	No	N/A

Table D.3
Identity Information-Trusts

Table D.3 shows the type of identity information (settlors and beneficiaries) required to be held by governmental authorities (**column 2**), resident trustee of a domestic trust (**column 3**), resident trustee of a foreign trust (**column 4**) and service providers, including banks, trust service providers and other persons (**column 5**).

Explanation of columns 2 through 6

The term "governmental authority" (column 2) includes trust registries, regulatory authorities and tax authorities. Columns 3 and 4 refer to trustees providing trustee services on a non-commercial basis. Requirements on such resident trustees to keep identity information would normally arise under either applicable trust law or under anti-money laundering legislation covering trustees generally. The requirement on professional service providers to keep identity information (column 5) typically arises under either specific laws regulating the business of managing trusts or under applicable anti-money laundering laws or under both. Some explanatory comments are provided for some of the countries in **column 6**.

Table D.3   Identity Information-Trusts

1	2	3	4	5	6
Country of residence of trustee and type of trust (if necessary)	**Identity information required to be held by:**				
	Governmental Authority a) settlor b) beneficiaries	**Trustee of Domestic Trust** a) settlor b) beneficiaries	**Trustee of Foreign Trust** a) settlor b) beneficiaries	**Service provider or other person** a) settlor b) beneficiaries	**Notes**
Andorra	N/A	N/A	N/A	N/A	
Anguilla	No*	a, b	a, b	a, b	*Public mutual funds established as unit trusts must provide identity information on trustees, managers, administrators, investment advisers *etc.*
Antigua and Barbuda	No information.	No information.	No information.	No information.	
Aruba	N/A	N/A	N/A*	N/A	*A foreign trust with a resident trustee is not recognised in Aruba.
Argentina	a, b	a, b	a, b	a, b	
Australia	b*	a, b**	a, b*	b	*For tax purposes. **For tax and common law purposes.
Austria	N/A	N/A	For tax purposes a resident trustee may be asked to provide evidence of the fiduciary relationship and information on settlor and beneficiaries to avoid being taxed on the trust income.	N/A	
The Bahamas	No	Yes, for common law purposes.	Yes, for common law purposes.	a, b	
Bahrain *Financial Trust*	a,b	a,b	No	a,b

The Financial Trust Law requires the information to be held. In addition, anti-money laundering customer due diligence requirements apply. | |

Table D.3   Identity Information-Trusts

1	2	3	4	5	6
Country of residence of trustee and type of trust (if necessary)	Identity information required to be held by:				Notes
	Governmental Authority a) settlor b) beneficiaries	Trustee of Domestic Trust a) settlor b) beneficiaries	Trustee of Foreign Trust a) settlor b) beneficiaries	Service provider or other person a) settlor b) beneficiaries	
Barbados	Yes*	a, b	a, b	For tax purposes a resident trustee may be asked to provide evidence of the fiduciary relationship and information on settlor and beneficiaries to avoid being taxed on the trust income.	*Where non-charitable purpose trusts. (a, b) and resident trustees subject to income tax (a, b).
Belgium	No*	N/A*	For tax purposes a resident trustee may be asked to provide evidence of the fiduciary relationship and information on settlor and beneficiaries to avoid being taxed on the trust income.	N/A	*Unless the assets of the foreign trust involve Belgian immovable property. *Belgium has no domestic trust legislation, but its laws regulate certain aspects of foreign trusts.
Belize	No*	a, b	No	a, b	*Public mutual funds established as unit trusts must provide identity information on trustees, managers, administrators, investment advisers *etc.*
Bermuda	No*	a, b	a, b The trustee would be governed by the laws of the jurisdiction of the trust but will be subject to anti-money laundering due diligence requirements where a trustee provides trustee services in or from Bermuda.	a, b	*Public mutual funds established as unit trusts must provide identity information on trustees, managers, administrators, investment advisers *etc.*
British Virgin Islands	No*	a, b	a, b	a, b	*Public mutual funds established as unit trusts must provide identity information on trustees, managers, administrators, investment advisers *etc.*
Brunei	No	No	No information.	No information.	

Table D.3   Identity Information-Trusts

1	2	3	4	5	6
Country of residence of trustee and type of trust (if necessary)	**Identity information required to be held by:**				
	Governmental Authority a) settlor b) beneficiaries	**Trustee of Domestic Trust** a) settlor b) beneficiaries	**Trustee of Foreign Trust** a) settlor b) beneficiaries	**Service provider or other person** a) settlor b) beneficiaries	**Notes**
Canada	a, b*	a, b*	a, b*	a, b*	*Where required for tax purposes.
Cayman Islands	No*	a, b	a, b	a, b	*Public mutual funds established as unit trusts must provide identity information on trustees, managers, administrators, investment advisers *etc.*
China	No	a, b	The trustee would have to comply with the laws of the country governing the trust.	No	
Cook Islands	No	a, b	The trustee would have to comply with the laws of the country governing the trust.	a, b	
Costa Rica	a, b	a, b	No	Banks and financial institutions that act as trustees must satisfy know your customer requirements of anti-money laundering.	
Cyprus	No*	a, b	a, b	a, b	*Public mutual funds established as unit trusts under the Mutual Funds Act must provide identity information on trustees, managers, administrators, investment advisers *etc.*
Czech Republic	N/A	N/A	No	N/A	
Denmark	N/A	N/A	a and b if required for tax purposes. Also, if carrying on a business activity in Denmark, the Book-keeping Act would normally require this information be kept.	N/A	
Dominica	No	a, b	a, b	a, b	

Table D.3   Identity Information-Trusts

1	2	3	4	5	6
Country of residence of trustee and type of trust (if necessary)	Identity information required to be held by:				
	Governmental Authority a) settlor b) beneficiaries	Trustee of Domestic Trust a) settlor b) beneficiaries	Trustee of Foreign Trust a) settlor b) beneficiaries	Service provider or other person a) settlor b) beneficiaries	Notes
Finland	N/A	N/A	Obligation to give such information if required by tax administration.	N/A	
France	N/A	N/A	N/A*	N/A	*A foreign trust with a resident trustee is not recognised in France.
Germany	N/A	N/A	For tax purposes a resident trustee may be asked to provide evidence of the fiduciary relationship and information on settlor and beneficiaries to avoid being taxed on the trust income.	N/A	
Gibraltar	Yes*	a, b	No	a, b	*Where the trust derives taxable income.
Greece	N/A	N/A	The trustee would have to comply with the laws of the country governing the trust.	N/A	
Grenada	No	No information.	No information.	No information.	
Guatemala	No	No	Trustee would have to comply with the laws of the country that govern the trust.	No	

Table D.3   Identity Information-Trusts

1	2	3	4	5	6
Country of residence of trustee and type of trust (if necessary)	Identity information required to be held by:				Notes
	Governmental Authority a) settlor b) beneficiaries	Trustee of Domestic Trust a) settlor b) beneficiaries	Trustee of Foreign Trust a) settlor b) beneficiaries	Service provider or other person a) settlor b) beneficiaries	
Guernsey	Yes*	a, b	a, b**	a, b	*Where the trustee is liable to tax because the trust has resident beneficiaries or is in receipt of Guernsey source income. Moreover, collective investment funds established as unit trusts must provide identity information on trustees, managers, administrators, investment advisers *etc.* to the GSFC (the financial services regulator). **For tax and anti-money laundering purposes.
Hong Kong, China	No	No	No	No	
Hungary	N/A	N/A	N/A	N/A	
Iceland	N/A	N/A	N/A	N/A	A foreign trust with a resident trustee is not recognised in Iceland.
Ireland	a, b*	a, b	a, b*	See footnote 1.	*For tax purposes.
Isle of Man	Yes*	a, b	Trustee would be governed by the laws of the jurisdiction of the trust.	Persons whose business includes acting as trustee must be registered and are subject to Fiduciary Services Act. As such they are subject to the anti-money laundering legislation and must comply with know your customer requirements.	*Where the trustee is liable to tax because the trust has resident beneficiaries or is in receipt of Isle of Man source income. Moreover, public mutual funds established as unit trusts must provide identity information on trustees, managers, administrators, investment advisers *etc.* Charitable trusts must also provide identity information to a Government Authority.

Table D.3 Identity Information-Trusts

1	2	3	4	5	6
Country of residence of trustee and type of trust (if necessary)	**Identity information required to be held by:**				
	Governmental Authority a) settlor b) beneficiaries	**Trustee of Domestic Trust** a) settlor b) beneficiaries	**Trustee of Foreign Trust** a) settlor b) beneficiaries	**Service provider or other person** a) settlor b) beneficiaries	**Notes**
Italy	a, b*	N/A	No**	N/A	*Identity information is already held for assets of trusts established under foreign law which are subject to registration under domestic law. The possibility and the ways in which the tax administration holds information about the beneficiaries and settlor/s will depend on the provisions implementing the 2007 Budget Law that established the relevance of foreign trusts for certain tax purposes. **However, anti-money laundering due diligence requirements may apply.
Japan	a, b*	a, b	a, b	Financial institutions providing services to trusts are subject to customer due diligence.	*For tax purposes.
Jersey	Yes*	a, b	Trustee would be governed by the laws of the jurisdiction of the trust but will be subject to anti-money laundering due diligence requirements.	Persons whose business includes acting as trustee must be registered and are subject to anti-money laundering due diligence requirements.	*For domestic trusts subject to tax in Jersey. Moreover, collective investment funds established as unit trusts must provide identity information on trustees, managers, administrators, investment advisers *etc.*
Korea	Yes*	a, b	a, b	Financial institutions providing services to trusts are subject to customer due diligence.	*Trustees are obliged to report identity information under the Real Name Financial Transaction Act.

Table D.3   Identity Information-Trusts

1	2	3	4	5	6
Country of residence of trustee and type of trust (if necessary)	Identity information required to be held by:				
	Governmental Authority a) settlor b) beneficiaries	Trustee of Domestic Trust a) settlor b) beneficiaries	Trustee of Foreign Trust a) settlor b) beneficiaries	Service provider or other person a) settlor b) beneficiaries	Notes
Liechtenstein	No	No	No	a, b Service providers, other than licensed trustees, covered by anti-money laundering rules may also hold information on settlors and beneficiaries where they engage in relevant business contact with the trust/trustee (e.g. a bank opening an account for the trust).	
Luxembourg	N/A	N/A	No	N/A	
Macao, China	a,b	a, b	a, b	a, b In addition, financial institutions providing services to trusts are subject to customer due diligence requirements.	Decree-Law 58/99/M, 18 Oct.
Malaysia	No	No information.	No information.	b	
Malta	a*,b**	a, b	a, b	See footnote 1.	* Disclosure is optional. **When required for tax purposes.
Marshall Islands	N/A	N/A	No	Financial institutions are required by anti-money laundering rules to know their customers (includes beneficiaries in the case of a trust).	
Mauritius	a,b	a, b*	a, b	a, b	*All trusts must appoint a qualified trustee (a licensed trust service provider) who must comply with anti-money laundering procedures).
Mexico	a, b	a, b	a, b	Only authorised financial institutions can act as a trustee of a domestic trust and must have information on settlors and beneficiaries.	

Table D.3   Identity Information-Trusts

1	2	3	4	5	6
Country of residence of trustee and type of trust (if necessary)	Identity information required to be held by:				
	Governmental Authority a) settlor b) beneficiaries	Trustee of Domestic Trust a) settlor b) beneficiaries	Trustee of Foreign Trust a) settlor b) beneficiaries	Service provider or other person a) settlor b) beneficiaries	Notes
Monaco	a, b*	N/A*	a, b*	a, b*	*Monaco has no domestic trust law, but recognises foreign trusts.
Montserrat	No*	No	No	a, b	*Mutual funds established as unit trusts must provide identity information on promoters, managers, administrators and custodian *etc*.
Nauru	No	a, b	a, b	Financial institutions including trust and company service providers are required to verify their customers' identity.	
Netherlands	N/A	N/A	a, b*	N/A	*Book-keeping requirements applicable to trustees will normally result in trustees being required to have identity information on the settlor and beneficiaries.
Netherlands Antilles	N/A	N/A	The trustee would be governed by the laws of the jurisdiction of the trust.	A service provider is under a general obligation to establish the identity of a customer before rendering any financial service.	
New Zealand	a, b*	a, b*	a, b*	Financial institutions are required by anti-money laundering legislation to "know your customer" (does not currently include beneficiaries).	*For tax purposes.
Niue	a, b	a, b	a, b	Financial institutions including trustee business are required to verify their customers' identity.	

Table D.3   Identity Information-Trusts

1	2	3	4	5	6
Country of residence of trustee and type of trust (if necessary)	**Identity information required to be held by:**				
	Governmental Authority a) settlor b) beneficiaries	**Trustee of Domestic Trust** a) settlor b) beneficiaries	**Trustee of Foreign Trust** a) settlor b) beneficiaries	**Service provider or other person** a) settlor b) beneficiaries	**Notes**
Norway	N/A	N/A	The book-keeping Act requires businesses to record the counter-party of every transaction. This would normally lead to the trustee being required to have identity information on the settlor and beneficiaries.	N/A	
Panama	a, b*	a, b	a, b	A license is required to conduct the business of acting as a trustee. Fiduciary companies are required to apply anti-money laundering Know Your Customer Policies.	*For tax purposes.
Philippines	b*	a, b	a, b	Financial institutions covered by the Anti-Money Laundering Act are required to verify customer identification.	*Where required for tax purposes.
Poland	N/A	N/A	No information.	N/A	
Portugal	N/A	N/A	Anti –money laundering know your customer requirements apply to the trustee. If information about settlors, protectors, enforcers and/or beneficiaries is necessary for Portuguese tax purposes, the trustee has a requirement to disclose such information to the tax authorities.	N/A	

Table D.3 Identity Information-Trusts

1	2	3	4	5	6
Country of residence of trustee and type of trust (if necessary)	Identity information required to be held by:				Notes
	Governmental Authority a) settlor b) beneficiaries	Trustee of Domestic Trust a) settlor b) beneficiaries	Trustee of Foreign Trust a) settlor b) beneficiaries	Service provider or other person a) settlor b) beneficiaries	
Russian Federation	N/A	N/A	For tax purposes a person who acts in a fiduciary capacity is required to maintain separate analytical records that make it possible to identify the principal and the beneficiary of the fiduciary agreement.	Anti-money laundering legislation requires legal and accounting service providers to carry out customer due diligence.	
Saint Kitts and Nevis	No	a, b	Trustee would have to comply with the laws of the country that govern the trust.	a, b	
Saint Lucia	a*	a, b	a, b	a, b	*The registration requirements apply only to international trusts. Mutual funds established as unit trusts under the Mutual Funds Act must provide identity information on promoters, managers, administrators and custodian *etc.*
Saint Vincent and the Grenadines	a*	No	No	a, b	*For international trusts, settlor information is always kept with the Authority. A trust deed is not registered unless it is signed and sealed by the settlor (original signature required). Information concerning the identity of beneficiaries may be submitted to the authorities and in practice this usually occurs. Public, private and accredited mutual funds established as unit trusts must provide identity information on trustees and settlors.

Table D.3   Identity Information-Trusts

1	2	3	4	5	6
Country of residence of trustee and type of trust (if necessary)	Identity information required to be held by:				Notes
	Governmental Authority a) settlor b) beneficiaries	Trustee of Domestic Trust a) settlor b) beneficiaries	Trustee of Foreign Trust a) settlor b) beneficiaries	Service provider or other person a) settlor b) beneficiaries	
Samoa	No	a, b	a, b	Anti-money laundering legislation imposes know your customer requirements on any person whose regular occupation or business is carrying out of trust business.	
San Marino	a, b	a, b	a, b	a, b	
Seychelles	No	a, b	No*	a, b	*Anti-money laundering legislation being revised to require corporate service providers (including those acting as nominees) to identify the settlors and beneficiaries.
Singapore	a, b*	a, b**	a, b**	Persons engaged in the business of acting as a trustee are required to be licensed unless exempt. Anti-money laundering and counter financing of terrorism (AML/CFT) legislation and guidelines require licensed persons to conduct customer due diligence.	*Unit and business trusts which are offered to retail or sophisticated investors and when required for tax purposes. **When required for tax purposes.
Slovak Republic	N/A	N/A	No information.	N/A	
South Africa	a,b	a,b	No*	a,b	*The Act is silent on the issue.
Spain	N/A	N/A	N/A*	N/A	*A foreign trust with a resident trustee is not recognised in Spain.

Table D.3 Identity Information-Trusts

1	2	3	4	5	6
Country of residence of trustee and type of trust (if necessary)	Identity information required to be held by:				Notes
	Governmental Authority a) settlor b) beneficiaries	Trustee of Domestic Trust a) settlor b) beneficiaries	Trustee of Foreign Trust a) settlor b) beneficiaries	Service provider or other person a) settlor b) beneficiaries	
Sweden	N/A	N/A	If information is considered necessary for Swedish tax assessment purposes, the taxpayer has a requirement to disclose such information to the tax authorities. This may concern information about settlors, protectors, enforcers and/or beneficiaries. All entities which carry on business in Sweden, which would include trustee activities, are also obliged to maintain accounting records.	N/A	
Switzerland	N/A	N/A	a, b	N/A	
Turkey	N/A	N/A	No information.	N/A	
Turks and Caicos Islands	No*	a, b	a, b	a, b	*Public mutual funds established as unit trusts must provide identity information on trustees, managers, administrators, investment advisers *etc.*
United Arab Emirates	No	a,b	a,b	a,b	The DIFC's trust law requires that a trustee identify the settlor and beneficiaries. (A trust service provider must at all times have verified documentary evidence of the settlors, trustees, beneficiaries and any person entitled who receives a distribution.)
United Kingdom	a, b*	a, b	a, b*	See footnote 1.	*When required for tax purposes.
United States	a, b*	a, b*	a, b*	Anti-money laundering due diligence requirements apply.	*For tax purposes.

Table D.3   Identity Information-Trusts

1	2	3	4	5	6
Country of residence of trustee and type of trust (if necessary)	Identity information required to be held by:				Notes
	Governmental Authority a) settlor b) beneficiaries	Trustee of Domestic Trust a) settlor b) beneficiaries	Trustee of Foreign Trust a) settlor b) beneficiaries	Service provider or other person a) settlor b) beneficiaries	
United States Virgin Islands	a, b*	a, b*	a, b*	Anti-money laundering due diligence requirements apply.	*For tax purposes.
Uruguay	a, b*	a, b	No	a, b**	*Registration is required for trusts to have effect vis a vis third parties. **Professional trustees are required to be registered with the Central Bank and must be able to make available to the authorities details of the capital settled in trusts under their management along with the identity of settlors and beneficiaries.
Vanuatu	No	a, b*	a, b*	a, b	*There are no private trustees in Vanuatu. A person carrying on a business as a trustee is deemed to be a financial institution and is therefore required to verify customer identity (settlor and beneficiaries, where ascertainable) where the amount of the transaction conducted through the financial institution exceeds VT 1 million.

[1] Laws that EU Member States have put in place to give effect to the Second Money Laundering Directive (2001/97/EC) provide a mechanism to identify settlors and beneficiaries of trusts. The Directive extends the customer identification, recordkeeping and reporting of suspicious transaction requirements which previously applied to credit and financial institutions to a range of professions including auditors, external accountants and tax advisers in the exercise of their professional activities as well as notaries and other independent legal advisers where they assist in the planning or execution of transactions for their clients, concerning among other things the creation, management or operation of trusts, companies or other similar structures. Pursuant to the Third Money Laundering Directive (2005/60/EC), which must be implemented in EU Member States by 15 December 2007, the range of persons covered by customer identification, record keeping and reporting requirements is further extended to include, among others, trust and company service providers. Moreover, customer due diligence requirements are expressly extended to beneficial owners, i.e. the natural persons who ultimately own or control the customer or on whose behalf a transaction or activity is being conducted.

Table D.4
Identity Information-Partnerships

Table D.4 shows the type of identity information required to be held by governmental authorities (**column 2**), at the partnership level (**column 3**) and by service providers, including banks, corporate service providers and other persons (**column 4**).

Explanation of columns 2 through 5

The term "governmental authority" (column 2) includes registries, regulatory authorities and tax authorities. The requirement on service providers (column 4) managing or providing services to a partnership to keep identity information typically arises under either specific laws regulating the service provider business or under applicable anti-money laundering laws or under both. Some explanatory comments are provided for some of the countries in **column 5**.

Table D.4 Identity Information-Partnerships

1	2	3	4	5
Country and type of partnership (if necessary)	Identity information required to be held by:			Special rules / Notes
	Governmental Authority	Partnership / partners	Service provider or other person	
Andorra	N/A	N/A	N/A	The concept of a partnership does not exist in Andorra.
Anguilla *Limited partnerships*	Yes (general partners only).*	Yes (both general and limited partners).	Anti-money laundering due diligence requirements apply.	*Limited partnerships engaged in an activity requiring a licence must report updated identity information on all partners.
Anguilla *General partnerships*	No*	No	Anti-money laundering due diligence requirements apply.	*General partnerships may only carry out business locally.
Antigua and Barbuda	No information.	No information.	No information.	
Aruba	Yes*	Yes	No**	*Such information must be provided under either commercial, regulatory or tax laws. **Legislation is on its way to address these aspects. Fiduciary service providers that are members of the Aruba Financial Center Association have agreed to voluntarily apply know your "know your customer" procedures.
Argentina	Yes*	Yes**	Yes**	*For commercial and tax purposes. **Only for tax purposes.
Australia	Yes*	Yes	No	*For tax purposes.
Austria	Yes	Yes	Anti-money laundering due diligence requirements apply.	
The Bahamas *Exempted limited partnerships*	Yes (general partners only).	Yes	Anti-money laundering due diligence requirements apply.	
The Bahamas *General partnerships*	No	Common law requirements apply.	Anti-money laundering due diligence requirements apply.	
Bahrain	Yes	Yes	Under Bahrain's anti-money laundering laws, financial businesses and certain designated non-financial business and professionals are required to undertake proper customer due diligence and maintain adequate customer identification records.	
Barbados *Limited partnerships*	Yes	No	No	

Table D.4   Identity Information-Partnerships

1	2	3	4	5
Country and type of partnership (if necessary)	Identity information required to be held by:			Special rules / Notes
	Governmental Authority	Partnership / partners	Service provider or other person	
Barbados *General partnerships*	Yes*	No	No	*For taxation purposes if doing business in Barbados.
Belgium	Yes*	Yes*	See footnote 1.	*Only foreign partnerships are considered here as all other such entities are treated as companies.
Belize *Limited liability partnerships*	Yes	Yes. The law requires that a partnership must keep at its registered office an updated list showing the name and address of each partner and indicating which of them is a designated partner.	Partnerships engaging in international financial services must be formed by a licensed service provider which is subject to know your customer requirements.	
Belize *General partnerships*	Yes*	Yes.		*For tax purposes if doing business in Belize.
Bermuda *Ordinary partnerships*	No	No	Anti-money laundering legislation requires banks, trust companies, deposit companies and regulated businesses to carry out customer due diligence.	
Bermuda *Exempted partnerships*	Yes	Yes	An exempted partnership and an overseas partnership must appoint a resident representative in Bermuda and maintain a registered office. If the representative has grounds to believe that the Minister's consent has not been obtained before a change of a general partner, he must report to the Minister. Non fulfilment of this duty is an offence. Anti-money laundering legislation requires banks, trust companies, deposit companies and regulated businesses to carry out customer due diligence.	"Exempted partnerships" are partnerships with one or more foreign partners and which have registered with the Registrar of Companies.

Table D.4   Identity Information-Partnerships

1	2	3	4	5
Country and type of partnership (if necessary)	**Identity information required to be held by:**			**Special rules / Notes**
	Governmental Authority	**Partnership / partners**	**Service provider or other person**	
Bermuda *Limited partnerships*	Yes (general partners only).	Yes	Anti-money laundering legislation requires banks, trust companies, deposit companies and regulated businesses to carry out customer due diligence.	
British Virgin Islands *Limited partnerships*	Yes (general partners only).	Yes	Anti-money laundering due diligence requirements apply.	Partnerships engaged in an activity requiring a licence must report updated identity information on all partners.
British Virgin Islands *General partnerships*	No	No		
Brunei *International partnerships*	Yes (general partners only).	Yes	International partnerships must be established by a trust corporation that must provide a certificate of due diligence prior to registration. Where a new partner is admitted an appropriate reaffirmation of the certificate specifying the nature of the change must be submitted to the Registrar.	
Brunei *Domestic partnerships*	No information.	No information.	No information.	
Canada	Yes	Yes	No	
Cayman Islands *(Exempt) limited partnership*	Yes (general partners only).	Yes	Anti-money laundering due diligence requirements apply	Public mutual funds established as partnerships under the Mutual Funds Law must provide identity information on trustees, managers, administrators, investment advisers etc.
Cayman Islands *General partnership*	No	Common law requirements apply.	Anti-money laundering due diligence requirements apply.	
China	Yes	Yes	No	
Cook Islands *Limited partnerships*	No	Yes	Anti-money laundering due diligence requirements apply.	
Cook Islands *International partnerships*	No			

Table D.4   Identity Information-Partnerships

1	2	3	4	5
Country and type of partnership (if necessary)	**Identity information required to be held by:**			**Special rules / Notes**
	Governmental Authority	**Partnership / partners**	**Service provider or other person**	
Cook Islands *General partnerships*	Yes			
Costa Rica	Yes*	Yes	No	*For tax purposes.
Cyprus	Yes	The General Partner of an investment limited partnership recognised by the Central Bank of Cyprus, is required to keep information on the identity of the limited partners.	See footnote 1.	
Czech Republic	N/A	N/A	N/A	Partnerships fall under the concept of companies in the Czech Republic.
Denmark	Yes*	Yes	See footnote 1.	*For VAT registration purposes.
Dominica	No information.	No information.	No information.	
Finland	Yes	Yes	See footnote 1.	
France	N/A	N/A	N/A	Partnerships fall under the concept of companies in France.
Germany *Civil partnership*	No*	Yes	See footnote 1.	*Unless civil partnership engages in business or otherwise requires a permit.
Germany *General and limited partnership*	Yes	Yes		
Gibraltar	Yes	Yes	Anti-money laundering due diligence requirements apply.	
Greece	N/A	N/A	N/A	Partnerships fall under the concept of companies in Greece.
Grenada	N/A	N/A	N/A	
Guatemala	Yes	No	No	
Guernsey *General partnerships*	Yes*	Yes	Service providers carrying on the activity of formation, management or administration of partnerships, are subject to anti-money laundering rules and must hold information on the identity of partners.	*Only identity of partners with a tax liability in Guernsey must be reported to the tax authorities.
Guernsey *Limited partnerships*	Yes (both general and limited partners).	Yes		
Hong Kong, China	Yes	No	No	

Table D.4   Identity Information-Partnerships

1	2	3	4	5
Country and type of partnership (if necessary)	**Identity information required to be held by:**			**Special rules / Notes**
	Governmental Authority	**Partnership / partners**	**Service provider or other person**	
Hungary	N/A	N/A	N/A	Partnerships fall under the concept of companies in Hungary.
Iceland	Yes*	Yes	Anti-money laundering know your customer requirements apply to certain service providers.	*Information on ownership registered with the District Commissioners and with Regional Tax Director for VAT purposes.
Ireland *General partnerships*	Yes*	No	See footnote 1.	*For tax purposes. A partnership which carries on business in Ireland must submit a tax return which includes information on partners' identities.
Ireland *Limited partnerships*	Yes*	Yes		*Both for commercial and tax purposes. A limited partnership which carries on business in Ireland must also submit a tax return which includes information on partners' identities.
Ireland *Investment Limited Partnership*	No	Yes*	See footnote 1.	*The general partner is a designated body for anti-money laundering purposes and must therefore identify and verify other partners.
Isle of Man *Limited partnerships*	Yes	Yes	Corporate Service Providers (which includes persons who carry on a business of forming partnerships) are required by anti-money laundering legislation to adhere to know your customer requirements.	
Isle of Man *General partnerships*	Yes*			*When required to lodge an income tax return.
Italy	Yes	Yes	See footnote 1.	
Japan	N/A	N/A	N/A	The concept of partnerships can fall under the concepts of companies and other relevant organisational structures in Japan.
Jersey	Yes*	Yes	Anti-money laundering legislation applies to relevant service providers who must apply know your customer rules.	*For commercial, regulatory and tax purposes. For limited partnerships a declaration has to be filed with the Registrar which will include the name and address of each general partner; for limited liability partnerships a declaration has to be filed with the Registrar which will include the names of all of the partners; and for general partnerships there is a requirement to provide the Registrar with the names of each of the individuals who are partners.
Korea	N/A	N/A	N/A	Partnerships fall under the concept of companies in Korea.

Table D.4 Identity Information-Partnerships

1	2	3	4	5
Country and type of partnership (if necessary)	**Identity information required to be held by:**			**Special rules / Notes**
	Governmental Authority	**Partnership / partners**	**Service provider or other person**	
Liechtenstein	Yes*	Yes	Yes. Liechtenstein anti-money laundering rules require that at least one person acting as an organ or director of a legal entity that does not conduct any commercial business in its country of domicile is obliged to identify and record the ultimate beneficial owner. Other service providers covered by anti-money laundering rules may also hold ownership information where they engage in relevant business contact with the partnership (e.g. a bank opening an account for the partnership).	*Special ownership disclosure requirements apply to banks, finance companies, investment undertakings, insurance companies and major holdings in publicly traded companies.
Luxembourg	Yes	Yes	See footnote 1.	
Macao, China	N/A	N/A	N/A	Partnerships fall under the concept of companies in Macao, China.
Malaysia	Yes (general partners).	Yes (both general and limited partners).	The anti-money laundering legislation requires virtually all persons managing or providing financial services to a partnership to perform customer due diligence.	
Malta	Yes*	Yes	See footnote 1.	*There are additional and more specific disclosure rules for limited partnerships that are used as collective investment funds.
Marshall Islands *General partnerships*	Yes*	Yes	Anti-money laundering know your customer requirements apply to financial institutions and cash dealers.	*Partnerships for professionals (attorneys, accountants) must be registered. When a potential customer requests to form a partnership and is not found in the relevant register, his/her credentials will be confirmed. If information cannot be confirmed or the potential customer is unknown, depending on the circumstances, the relevant register can refuse to form a partnership or ask for additional information, such as the name(s) of the beneficial owners.
Marshall Islands *Limited partnerships*	Yes* (general partners only).			
Mauritius	Yes*	Yes	Anti-money laundering due diligence requirements apply.	*Partnerships engaged in financial services sector are subject to special due diligence requirements.

Table D.4   Identity Information-Partnerships

1	2	3	4	5
Country and type of partnership (if necessary)	Identity information required to be held by:			Special rules / Notes
	Governmental Authority	Partnership / partners	Service provider or other person	
Mexico	Yes*	Yes	Mexico does not have special rules regarding the information that relevant service providers are compelled to keep regarding the identity or ownership of the parties involved in a partnership. However, relevant service providers are subject to general tax obligations regarding tax registration and keeping their accounting records and other relevant information for up to 5 years.	*For tax purposes and under FDI incentive rules.
Monaco	N/A	N/A		Partnerships fall within the concept of companies in Monaco.
Montserrat *Limited partnerships*	Yes* (general partners only).	No (other than for general partners in limited partnerships).	Anti-money laundering due diligence requirements apply.	*Partnerships engaged in an activity requiring a licence are subject to special due diligence requirements.
Montserrat *General partnerships*	No*			
Nauru	Yes	No	Financial institutions including trust and company service providers are required to verify their customers' identity.	
Netherlands	Yes	Yes	See footnote 1.	
Netherlands Antilles	Yes*(general partners only).	Yes (general partners only).	Anti-money laundering due diligence requirements apply.	*Such information must be provided under either commercial, regulatory or tax laws.
New Zealand	Yes	Yes	No	
Niue	Yes*	Yes	Pursuant to the Financial Transactions Report Act, financial institutions are required to verify their customers' identity.	*For commercial or tax purposes.
Norway	Yes	Yes	Anti-money laundering due diligence requirements apply.	
Panama	Yes*	Yes	Financial institutions, trusts companies and exchange and settlement houses are subject to know your customer requirements.	*Except for informal partnerships and economic interest groupings.
Philippines	Yes	Yes	Financial institutions covered by the Anti-Money Laundering Act are required to verify customer identification.	
Poland	Yes	Yes	See footnote 1.	

Table D.4   Identity Information-Partnerships

1	2	3	4	5
Country and type of partnership (if necessary)	**Identity information required to be held by:**			**Special rules / Notes**
	Governmental Authority	**Partnership / partners**	**Service provider or other person**	
Portugal	N/A*	N/A*	N/A*	*Partnerships fall under the general concept of companies in Portugal, but some special rules apply (for instance, a "transparency regime" for tax purposes which is mandatory for some types of companies).
Russian Federation	Yes	Yes	Anti-money laundering legislation requires legal and accounting service providers to carry out customer due diligence.	
Saint Kitts and Nevis *Limited partnerships (applicable only in Saint Kitts)*	Yes* (general partners only).	Yes	Anti-money laundering due diligence requirements apply.	*Limited partnerships engaged in an activity requiring a licence are subject to special due diligence requirements.
Saint Lucia	Yes	No	Anti-money laundering due diligence requirements apply.	
Saint Vincent and the Grenadines	Yes	Yes	Anti-money laundering due diligence requirements apply.*	*Partnerships carry out business only locally.
Samoa *Domestic partnerships*	Yes*	Yes	No	*For tax purposes.
Samoa *International and limited partnerships*	No		Registration of international and limited partnerships must be done through a trustee company which, pursuant to anti-money laundering legislation, is required to apply know your customer rules.**	**Anti-money laundering legislation applies when transaction exceeds $30,000.
San Marino	Yes	Yes	Anti-money laundering know your customer requirements apply to all credit and financial institutions. In the context of partnerships, the obligation to identify customers means that certified copies of the partnership agreement, of industry and commerce licenses, certification of persons representing the partnership must be supplied.	
Seychelles *General partnerships*	No	No	Anti-money laundering due diligence requirements apply.	
Seychelles *Limited partnerships*	Yes	Yes		

Table D.4   Identity Information-Partnerships

1	2	3	4	5
Country and type of partnership (if necessary)	Identity information required to be held by:			Special rules / Notes
	Governmental Authority	Partnership / partners	Service provider or other person	
Singapore	Yes	Yes	Anti-money laundering and counter financing of terrorism (AML/CFT) legislation and guidelines require persons providing financial, legal and accounting services to conduct customer due diligence.	
Slovak Republic	N/A	N/A	N/A	Partnerships fall under the concept of companies in the Slovak Republic.
South Africa	No	If there is a written agreement the partners would be identified in the agreement. The partners would normally know the identity of the other partners.*	Anti-money laundering customary due diligence requirements apply to certain service providers.	*Each time there is a change in partners, the partnership terminates.
Spain	N/A	N/A	N/A	Partnerships fall under the concept of companies in Spain.
Sweden	Yes	Yes	See footnote 1.	
Switzerland	Yes	Yes	Where service providers establish a contractual relationship with the partnership and perform a covered activity, anti-money laundering law requires the identification of beneficial owners (e.g. bank opening a bank account for a partnership).	
Turkey	Yes	Yes	Independent accountant and sworn-in financial advisors providing services to partnerships must perform customer due diligence.	
Turks and Caicos Islands *Limited partnerships*	Yes* (general partners only).	Yes	Only if the limited partner is a company.	*Limited partnerships engaged in an activity requiring a licence are subject to special identity reporting requirements.
Turks and Caicos Islands *General partnerships*	No information.	No information.	No information.	
United Arab Emirates *(DIFC) General partnerships Limited partnerships Limited liability partnerships*	Yes	Yes	Anti-money laundering legislation requires financial service providers to carry out customer due diligence.	

Table D.4   Identity Information-Partnerships

1	2	3	4	5
Country and type of partnership (if necessary)	Identity information required to be held by:			Special rules / Notes
	Governmental Authority	Partnership / partners	Service provider or other person	
United Arab Emirates *(DIFC) Partnership limited by shares*	Yes			
United Kingdom *General partnership*	Yes*	No	See footnote 1.	*Partnerships that carry on business in the UK are required to file a Partnership Tax Statement. The statement requires that the names and addresses of partners be disclosed.
United Kingdom *Limited partnership*	Yes*	Yes		*A limited partnership or limited liability partnership which carries on business in the UK must also submit a tax return which includes information on the partners' identities.
United Kingdom *Limited liability partnership*	Yes*	Yes		
United States	No	A partnership/LLC must produce a list of members to any other member on reasonable demand.	Anti-money laundering due diligence requirements apply.	
United States Virgin Islands *General partnerships*	Yes*	Yes	No information.	*For tax purposes. In the case of any partnership that does business in the USVI, a business license is required to be obtained. The application for such a license generally requires disclosure of the principles of the business and/or the persons responsible for the business operations in the USVI.
United States Virgin Islands *Limited partnerships*	Yes, the general partners.*	Yes	No	*Information on all partners is required for tax purposes. In the case of any partnership that does business in the USVI, a business license is required to be obtained. The application for such a license generally requires disclosure of the principles of the business and/or the persons responsible for the business operations in the USVI.
Uruguay *General partnerships*	Yes	Yes	Service providers covered by anti-money laundering rules should hold ownership information where they engage in relevant business contacts with the partnership.	
Uruguay *Limited partnerships*	Yes	Yes*		*Except where shares of limited partners are issued to bearer.

Table D.4   Identity Information-Partnerships

1	2	3	4	5
Country and type of partnership (if necessary)	**Identity information required to be held by:**			**Special rules / Notes**
	Governmental Authority	**Partnership / partners**	**Service provider or other person**	
Uruguay *Partnerships limited by shares*	Yes	Yes*		*Information regarding ownership of bearer shares is entered in the register of attendance at partnership meetings.
Vanuatu *General partnerships*	No	No	Anti-money laundering know your customer requirements apply to financial institutions where a person conducts a transaction through the institution with the partnership and the amount of the transaction exceeds VT 1 million.	
Vanuatu *Limited partnerships*	Yes	Yes		

[1] Laws that EU Member States have put in place to give effect to the Second Money Laundering Directive (2001/97/EC) provide a mechanism to identify partners of partnerships. The Directive extends the customer identification, recordkeeping and reporting of suspicious transaction requirements which previously applied to credit and financial institutions to a range of professions including auditors, external accountants and tax advisers in the exercise of their professional activities as well as notaries and other independent legal advisers where they assist in the planning or execution of transactions for their clients, concerning among other things the creation, management or operation of trusts, companies or other similar structures. Pursuant to the Third Money Laundering Directive (2005/60/EC), which must be implemented in EU Member States by 15 December 2007, the range of persons covered by customer identification, record keeping and reporting requirements is further extended to include, among others, trust and company service providers. Moreover, customer due diligence requirements are expressly extended to beneficial owners, i.e. the natural persons who ultimately own or control the customer or on whose behalf a transaction or activity is being conducted.

Table D.5
Identity Information-Foundations

Table D.5 shows the type of identity information (founders, beneficiaries and members of foundation council) required to be held by governmental authorities (**column 2**), at the foundation level (**column 3**) and by service providers, including banks, corporate service providers and other persons (**column 4**).

Explanation of columns 2 through 5

The term "governmental authority" (column 2) includes foundation registries, regulatory authorities and tax authorities. The requirement on service providers (column 4) managing or providing services to a foundation to keep identity information typically arises under either specific laws regulating the corporate service provider business or under applicable anti-money laundering laws or under both. Some explanatory comments are provided for some of the countries in **column 5**.

Table D.5   Identity Information-Foundations

1	2	3	4	5
Country and type of foundation (if necessary)	**Identity information required to be held by:**			**Special rules / Notes**
	Governmental Authority	**Foundation and members of the foundation council**	**Service provider or other person**	
	a) founders **b) members of foundation council** **c) beneficiaries (where applicable)**			
Argentina	a,b,c*	a,b,c**	No***	*For commercial and tax purposes. **For tax purposes. ***Service providers are obliged to give information on transactions with the foundation when the tax administration requests it.
Aruba	a, b, c*	a, b	a, b, c**	*The members of the Foundation Council must be disclosed to the Chamber of Commerce. Information about the founders and beneficiaries will have to be disclosed to the tax authorities. **The information is held by the public notary.
Austria	a, b	a, b*	See footnote 1.	*The members of the foundation council generally know the identity of the beneficiaries but there are cases where they only know the identity of the entity or person that decides on future beneficiaries).
The Bahamas	a, b	a, b	a, b* In addition service providers are required for anti-money laundering purposes to conduct customer due diligence including identification of beneficial owners.	*The secretary to the foundation must be a licensed service provider.
Belgium	a, b, c	a, b, c*	See footnote 1.	*In some cases.
Costa Rica	a, b	a, b	No information.	
Czech Republic	a, b	a, b, c*	See footnote 1.	*Apart from accounting and auditing obligations, in the annual report, beneficiary information must be stated if contributions exceed 10 000 CZK, unless the beneficiary obtains such contribution due to health or other humanitarian reasons and wishes to remain anonymous.
Denmark	a,b,c	a,b,c	See footnote 1.	
Finland	b	a, b, c	See footnote 1.	

Table D.5   Identity Information-Foundations

1	2	3	4	5
Country and type of foundation (if necessary)	**Identity information required to be held by:**			**Special rules / Notes**
	Governmental Authority	**Foundation and members of the foundation council**	**Service provider or other person**	
		a) founders **b) members of foundation council** **c) beneficiaries (where applicable)**		
France	b*	a, b	See footnote 1.	*Except in connection with the publication formalities involved in the transfer of real estate ownership, no information must be disclosed on the identity of the founders. However, the articles of association contain this information and may be consulted where the foundation's headquarters are located.
Germany	a, b, c	a, b	See footnote 1.	
Greece	No information.	No information.	No information (however see footnote 1).	
Guatemala	*	None*	*	*Required to register in the municipal register and submit copies of its foundation deed.
Hungary	a, b	a, b	See footnote 1.	
Italy	b	a, b, c	See footnote 1.	
Japan	a,b	a, b	Anti-money laundering legislation requires financial service providers to undertake customer due diligence.	
Korea	b	a, b	Anti-money laundering legislation requires financial service providers to undertake customer due diligence.	
Liechtenstein	a, b*	a, b, c**	Service providers covered by anti-money laundering rules may also be required to hold information on a), b), or c) where they engage in relevant business contact with the foundation (*e.g.* a bank opening an account for the foundation).	*Note that the register further contains information on the identity of any other person with authority to represent the foundation. **Liechtenstein anti-money laundering rules require that at least one person acting as an organ or director of the foundation that does not conduct any commercial business in Liechtenstein knows the identity of founders and beneficiaries (where applicable).
Luxembourg	No information.	b	See footnote 1.	

Table D.5   Identity Information-Foundations

1	2	3	4	5
Country and type of foundation (if necessary)	Identity information required to be held by:			Special rules / Notes
	Governmental Authority	Foundation and members of the foundation council	Service provider or other person	
		a) founders b) members of foundation council c) beneficiaries (where applicable)		
Macao, China	a,b	a,b	Anti-money laundering customer due diligence requirements apply to financial institutions	
Malta	b*	b*	b*	*Foundations, though recognised in case law and referred to in some laws, are not yet specifically regulated by legislation. Legislation to address this gap is in preparation. Existing foundations are registered for income tax purposes.
Mexico	a	a	Anti-money laundering legislation requires service providers to undertake customer due diligence. Mexico does not have special rules regarding the information that relevant service providers are compelled to keep regarding the identity or ownership of the parties involved in a foundation. However, relevant service providers are subject to general tax obligations regarding tax registration and keeping their accounting records and other relevant information for up to 5 years.	
Monaco	a, b	a, b	Anti-money laundering legislation requires service providers to identify a, b, c when engaged in relevant business contact with a foundation.	
Netherlands	a, b	a, b, c	See footnote 1.	
Netherlands Antilles	a, b	a, b	a, b, c*	*The information is held by the public notary.
Norway	a, b	a, b, c	Anti-money laundering legislation requires credit and financial institutions, fund managers, auditors and lawyers to identify their clients in relation to transactions amounting to NOK 100 000 or more.	
Panama	a, b, c*	a, b	All foundations must have a Resident Agent who is bound by know your customer rules and must keep sufficient information for the customer to be identified.	*Manner of designating beneficiaries.

Table D.5 Identity Information-Foundations

1	2	3	4	5
Country and type of foundation (if necessary)	Identity information required to be held by:			Special rules / Notes
	Governmental Authority	Foundation and members of the foundation council	Service provider or other person	
	a) founders b) members of foundation council c) beneficiaries (where applicable)			
Poland	b	No information.	See footnote 1.	
Portugal	a, b	a, b, c	See footnote 1.	
Russian Federation	No information.	No information.	No information.	
Saint Kitts and Nevis (applicable only in Nevis)	a, b, c	a, b, c	a, b, c*	*Information must be kept at the registered office which shall be the address of the registered agent in Nevis.
San Marino	a, b	a, b	Not applicable.	
Slovak Republic	a, b	a, b, c	See footnote 1.	
Spain	a, b	a, b	See footnote 1.	It is not possible to create a foundation to benefit individuals such as the members of a family. Foundations must be constituted without a lucrative goal to pursue a general interest aim.
Sweden	a, b	a, b, c	See footnote 1.	
Switzerland	a, b*	a, b	Where service providers establish a contractual relationship with the foundation and perform a covered activity, anti-money laundering law requires customer due diligence (e.g. bank managing the assets of the foundation).	*Only foundations other than family and ecclesiastical foundations (where registration with the Trade Register is optional).
Turkey	a	a	No information.	
Uruguay	a, b*	a, b*	Banks are required to perform customer due diligence.	*Beneficiaries may not be individually identified as foundations must have a general interest purpose.

[1] Laws that EU Member States have put in place to give effect to the Second Money Laundering Directive (2001/97/EC) provide a mechanism to identify founders and beneficiaries. The Directive extends the customer identification, recordkeeping and reporting of suspicious transaction requirements which previously applied to credit and financial institutions to a range of professions including auditors, external accountants and tax advisers in the exercise of their professional activities as well as notaries and other independent legal advisers where they assist in the planning or execution of transactions for their clients, concerning among other things the creation, management or operation of trusts, companies or other similar structures. Pursuant to the Third Money Laundering Directive (2005/60/EC), which must be implemented in EU Member States by 15 December 2007, the range of persons covered by customer identification, record keeping and reporting requirements is further extended to include, among others, trust and company service providers. Moreover, customer due diligence requirements are expressly extended to beneficial owners, i.e. the natural persons who ultimately own or control the customer or on whose behalf a transaction or activity is being conducted.

Table D.6
Accounting Information-Companies

This table shows for each of the countries reviewed the legal requirements relating to the nature of the accounting records that must be created and retained, specific requirements with respect to their auditing and lodgement with a governmental authority and the rules regarding the retention of the records.

Explanation of columns 2 through 7

Column 2 shows whether there is a specific requirement to keep accounting records. Where company directors have discretion as to the nature and extent of the accounting records that must be kept this has been categorised as not having a requirement to keep accounting records.

Column 3 shows the extent to which countries require accounting records to meet the standards as set out in the JAHGA paper, "Enabling Effective Exchange of Information: Availability Standard and Reliability Standard" (see Annex III of the Report). In this column the following code has been used (a) for "correctly explain the company's transactions", (b) for "enable the company's position to be determined with reasonable accuracy at any time", (c) for "allow financial statements to be prepared" and (d) for "include underlying documentation such as invoices, contracts, etc".

Column 4 shows which countries have a requirement to prepare financial statements.

Column 5 shows whether a requirement exists to file financial statements with a governmental authority and/or to file a tax return.

Column 6 indicates which countries have a requirement that financial statements be audited.

Column 7 sets out the applicable retention period.

Table D.6   Accounting Information-Companies

1	2	3	4	5	6	7
Country and type of company (if necessary)	Requirement to keep accounting records	Accounting records meet a, b, c, d*	Requirement to prepare financial statements	Requirement to file financial statements with a Governmental Authority and/or file a requisite tax return	Requirement to have financial statements audited	Retention period for accounting records
Andorra *Corporations and Limited liability companies*	Yes	Yes: a, b & c	Yes	No, except for financial institutions, insurance companies, public institutions, bingo companies and companies which benefit from public subsidies.	No, except for financial institutions, insurance companies, public institutions, bingo companies and companies which benefit from public subsidies.	10 years
Anguilla *Companies Act (public companies)*	Yes	Yes	Yes	Yes	Yes	6 years
Anguilla *Companies Act (private companies)*	Yes	Yes: a, b & d	No	No	No	6 years
Anguilla *International Business Companies Act*	Yes	Yes: a & b	No	No	No	6 years
Anguilla *Limited Liability Companies Act*	No	No	No	No	No	No
Antigua and Barbuda	Yes	No information.	No information.	No information.	No information.	No information.
Argentina	Yes	Yes	Yes	Yes	Yes	10 years
Aruba	Yes	Yes	Yes	Yes	Yes, for public companies, regulated activities and companies qualifying for certain tax regimes.	10 years
Australia	Yes	Yes	Yes	Yes, subject to threshold test	Yes, subject to threshold test.	7 years
Austria	Yes	Yes	Yes	Yes	Yes, for joint-stock company, and a certain type of limited liability company.	7 years

Table D.6   Accounting Information-Companies

1	2	3	4	5	6	7
Country and type of company (if necessary)	Requirement to keep accounting records	Accounting records meet a, b, c, d*	Requirement to prepare financial statements	Requirement to file financial statements with a Governmental Authority and/or file a requisite tax return	Requirement to have financial statements audited	Retention period for accounting records
The Bahamas	Only for public companies and regulated companies in the banking, securities and insurance sectors.	Yes, for public companies and regulated companies in the banking, securities and insurance sectors.	Yes, for public companies and regulated companies in the banking, securities and insurance sectors.	Public companies and regulated companies in the banking, securities and insurance sectors are required to file audited financial statements with the relevant regulator.	Yes, for public companies and regulated companies in the banking, securities and insurance sectors.	7 years for public companies and regulated companies in the securities industry.
Bahrain	Yes	Yes	Yes	Yes	Yes	10 year (5 years for records and supporting materials).
Barbados	Yes	Yes	Yes, unless exempted.	Yes, every public company carrying on business is required to prepare and lodge with the Commissioner audited financial statements, and every private company required to file income tax returns. Financial institutions shall report to the Government Regulators.	Yes, unless exempted.	Indefinite, however permission can be granted after 9 years to dispose of certain records.
Belgium	Yes	Yes	Yes	Yes	Yes, with some exemptions for small companies.	10 years
Belize *Companies Act*	Yes	Yes	No	No	Yes when a company opts to submit an income tax return.	6 years
Belize *International Business companies*	No, unless directors consider it necessary or desirable.	No, unless engaged in a regulated activity or when directors consider it necessary or desirable.	No	No	No, unless engaged in a regulated activity.	No

Table D.6 Accounting Information-Companies

1	2	3	4	5	6	7
Country and type of company (if necessary)	Requirement to keep accounting records	Accounting records meet a, b, c, d*	Requirement to prepare financial statements	Requirement to file financial statements with a Governmental Authority and/or file a requisite tax return	Requirement to have financial statements audited	Retention period for accounting records
Bermuda	Yes	Yes	Yes, but private companies may waive laying of financial statements for a particular interval if all the members and directors agree in writing or at an annual general meeting unless the company carries on a regulated financial services activity and is required to prepare financial statements.	No	Yes, but private companies may waive appointment of an auditor until the next annual meeting if all the members and directors agree in writing or at the annual meeting unless the company carries on a regulated financial services activity and is required to audit its accounts.	6 years
British Virgin Islands *Companies Act*	Yes	Yes	Yes, for public companies.	Yes	No	5 years
British Virgin Islands *International Business Companies Act and BVI Business Companies Act*	Yes	Yes: a & b	No	Yes	No	5 years
Brunei *Domestic companies*	Yes	Yes: a, b, & c	Yes	Yes	Yes	No information.
Brunei *International companies*	No, unless directors consider it necessary or desirable.	No, unless engaged in a regulated activity or when directors consider it necessary or desirable.	No	No	No	None
Canada	Yes	Yes	Yes	Yes.	Yes, in some circumstances.	6 years
Cayman Islands	Yes	Yes	No, except for regulated activities.	No, except for regulated activities.	No, except for regulated activities.	5 years

Table D.6   Accounting Information-Companies

1	2	3	4	5	6	7
Country and type of company (if necessary)	Requirement to keep accounting records	Accounting records meet a, b, c, d*	Requirement to prepare financial statements	Requirement to file financial statements with a Governmental Authority and/or file a requisite tax return	Requirement to have financial statements audited	Retention period for accounting records
China	Yes	Yes	Yes	Yes	Yes, for listed corporations and certain foreign investment enterprises.	10 years
Cook Islands *Companies Act*	Yes	Yes	Yes	Yes	Yes, for public companies.	7 years
Cook Islands *International Companies Act*	Yes	Yes	No, except for regulated activities.	No, except for regulated activities.	No, except for regulated activities.	No
Costa Rica	Yes	Yes	No	Yes	No	4 years
Cyprus	Yes	Yes	No	Yes, a tax return must be filed.	No	7 years
Czech Republic	Yes	Yes	Yes	Yes	Yes, depends on the economic size of a company.	5 years (10 years for financial statements and annual reports).
Denmark	Yes	Yes	Yes	Yes	Yes	5 years
Dominica *Companies Act*	Yes	No information.	No information.	No information.	No information.	No information.
Dominica *International Business Companies Act*	Yes	Yes: a & b All a, b, c & d for companies engaged in an activity requiring a license.	No, except for companies engaged in an activity requiring a license.	No, except for companies engaged in an activity requiring a license.	No, except for companies engaged in an activity requiring a license.	No information.
Finland	Yes	Yes	Yes	Yes	Yes	10 years
France	Yes	Yes	Yes	Yes	Yes, for public limited liability companies, simplified joint-stock companies and natural/legal persons which cross a certain threshold turnover.	10 years
Germany	Yes	Yes	Yes	Yes	Yes, with an exception for small companies.	10 years
Gibraltar	Yes	Yes	Yes	Yes	Yes, subject to threshold test.	5 years

Table D.6 Accounting Information-Companies

1	2	3	4	5	6	7
Country and type of company (if necessary)	Requirement to keep accounting records	Accounting records meet a, b, c, d*	Requirement to prepare financial statements	Requirement to file financial statements with a Governmental Authority and/or file a requisite tax return	Requirement to have financial statements audited	Retention period for accounting records
Greece	Yes	Yes	Yes	Yes	Yes	6 years
Grenada *Companies Act*	Yes	Yes	Yes	Yes	No information.	No information.
Grenada *International Companies Act*	Yes	Yes: a & b	No	No	No	7 years for anti-money laundering purposes.
Guatemala	Yes	Yes	Yes, with exceptions for small business.	Yes	No	5 years
Guernsey	Yes	Yes: a, b, c & d	Yes	Yes, companies that are in receipt of income liable to tax in Guernsey must submit a tax return. Also regulated financial services businesses including open-ended collective investment funds and closed-ended collective investment funds must provide their financial statements to the Guernsey Financial Services Commission.	Yes, except for asset holding companies that specifically elect for unaudited status.	6 years, but, for income tax purposes, with effect from January 2007 companies that carry on a business or receive income from the letting of property must retain their records for 6 years after the end of the year in which the relevant income tax return was submitted.
Hong Kong, China	Yes	Yes	Yes	Yes	Yes	7 years
Hungary	Yes	Yes	Yes	Yes	Yes, with exceptions for small companies.	8/10 years
Iceland	Yes	Yes	Yes	Yes	Yes	7 years
Ireland	Yes	Yes	Yes	Yes, companies liable to tax must file returns. Limited companies are required to file accounts with the Registrar of Companies.	Yes, with exceptions for small companies.	6 years

Table D.6   Accounting Information-Companies

1	2	3	4	5	6	7
Country and type of company (if necessary)	Requirement to keep accounting records	Accounting records meet a, b, c, d*	Requirement to prepare financial statements	Requirement to file financial statements with a Governmental Authority and/or file a requisite tax return	Requirement to have financial statements audited	Retention period for accounting records
Isle of Man	Yes	Yes	Yes, although companies incorporated under the Companies Act 2006 must only keep reliable accounting records at the office of the registered agent.	Yes, an income tax return required where liable to pay tax. Public companies are required to lodge accounts with the Companies registry.	Yes, companies other than limited liability companies and companies incorporated under the Companies Act 2006 are required to be audited. Certain companies may elect to dispense with an audit.	6 years for public companies and companies incorporated under the Companies Act 2006, and 3 years for private companies.
Italy	Yes	Yes	Yes	Yes	Yes	10 years
Japan	Yes	Yes	Yes	Yes	Yes, for a certain joint-stock company.	10 years
Jersey	Yes	Yes: a, b, c & d	Yes	Yes, resident companies and non resident companies carrying on business in Jersey or which are in receipt of income from sources in Jersey are liable to tax and must submit a tax return. Public companies and private companies deemed to be public are required to file accounts with the Registrar of companies. Financial institutions shall report to the Financial Services Commission.	Yes for public companies and private companies that adopt the standard table unless a majority of members decide against it.	10 years
Korea	Yes	Yes	Yes	Yes	Yes, for a certain joint-stock company.	10 years
Liechtenstein	Yes	Yes	Yes	Yes	Yes	10 years
Luxembourg	Yes	Yes	Yes	Yes	Yes, except for small business.	10 years

Table D.6 Accounting Information-Companies

1	2	3	4	5	6	7
Country and type of company (if necessary)	Requirement to keep accounting records	Accounting records meet a, b, c, d*	Requirement to prepare financial statements	Requirement to file financial statements with a Governmental Authority and/or file a requisite tax return	Requirement to have financial statements audited	Retention period for accounting records
Macao, China	Yes	Yes	Yes	Yes	Yes, except for private companies.	10 years
Malaysia	Yes	Yes	Yes	Yes	Yes, other than for Labuan companies not undertaking regulated activities.	7 years
Malta	Yes	Yes	Yes	Yes	Yes	10 years
Marshall Islands *Resident domestic corporations*	Yes	Yes	No, however, a certain shareholder can request that financial statements be prepared.	Yes	No, except for banks and publicly traded companies.	3 years
Marshall Islands *Non-resident domestic corporations and Limited Liability Companies*	Yes	Yes: a, b & c	No	No	No, except for banks and publicly traded companies.	No
Mauritius *Local companies*	Yes	Yes	Yes	Yes	Yes, with an exception for small private companies.	7 years
Mauritius *Category 1 Global Business Companies*	Yes	Yes	Yes	Yes	Yes	7 years
Mauritius *Category 2 Global Business Companies*	No, but they should keep such accounting records as the directors consider necessary or desirable.	No	No	No	No	7 years
Mexico	Yes	Yes	Yes	Yes	Yes, subject to threshold tests and in other specified circumstances.	5 years

Table D.6 Accounting Information-Companies

1	2	3	4	5	6	7
Country and type of company (if necessary)	Requirement to keep accounting records	Accounting records meet a, b, c, d*	Requirement to prepare financial statements	Requirement to file financial statements with a Governmental Authority and/or file a requisite tax return	Requirement to have financial statements audited	Retention period for accounting records
Monaco	Yes	Yes	Yes	Yes for stock companies (public or not) so called SA companies and all companies subject to profit tax.	Yes, for stock companies.	10 years
Montserrat *Companies Act*	Yes	Yes	Yes	Yes, for public companies and private companies with gross revenue above a certain threshold.	Yes, for public companies.	Not specified but 6 years for anti-money laundering purposes.
Montserrat *Limited Liability Companies Act*	No	No	No	No	No	No
Montserrat *International Business Companies Act*	Yes	Yes: a & b	No	No	No	No
Nauru	Yes	Yes	No, only when requested by a company member.	No	No, only when requested by a company member.	6 years
Netherlands	Yes	Yes	Yes	Yes	Yes	7 years
Netherlands Antilles	Yes	Yes	Yes	Yes	Yes for public companies and regulated activities.	10 years
New Zealand	Yes	Yes	Yes	Yes	Yes (however in certain circumstances the shareholders can, by unanimous resolution, agree that no auditor be appointed).	7 years
Niue *Domestic companies*	Yes	Yes	Yes	Yes	Yes, except in the case of private companies.	7 years
Niue *International Business Companies*	Yes	No	No	No	No	No

Table D.6   Accounting Information-Companies

1	2	3	4	5	6	7
Country and type of company (if necessary)	Requirement to keep accounting records	Accounting records meet a, b, c, d*	Requirement to prepare financial statements	Requirement to file financial statements with a Governmental Authority and/or file a requisite tax return	Requirement to have financial statements audited	Retention period for accounting records
Norway	Yes	Yes	Yes	Yes	Yes	3, 5 or 10 years depending on type of document.
Panama	Yes, if business undertaken in Panama.	Yes, if business undertaken in Panama.	Yes, if trading entity.	Yes, a tax return is required for all companies with Panamanian source income.	No, except for regulated entities.	5 years
Philippines	Yes	Yes	Yes	Yes	Yes, for corporations of a certain size.	A minimum of 3 years and up to 10 years in the case of fraud.
Poland	Yes	Yes	Yes	Yes	Yes, for joint stock companies, and limited liability companies which satisfy criteria.	Permanently for approved financial statements; 5 years for other files.
Portugal	Yes	Yes	Yes	Yes	Yes, for joint-stock companies, limited liability companies that meet a threshold test, and holding companies.	10 years
Russian Federation	Yes	Yes	No	Yes, all companies must file an annual tax return.	Yes, for open joint-stock companies, banks, insurance companies, stock exchanges and investment institutions. Other companies subject to threshold tests.	4 years
Saint Kitts and Nevis	Yes	Yes	Yes	Yes, except for exempt companies incorporated under the Saint Kitts Companies Act.	Yes, for public companies and regulated activities.	12 years under the Saint Kitts Companies Act.
Saint Kitts and Nevis *Nevis Business Corporation Ordinance*	Yes	Yes	Yes	Yes, in respect of those Nevis Business Corporations (NBCs) which carry on financial services business.	Yes in respect of those NBCs which carry on financial services business.	5 years under anti-money laundering regulations.

Table D.6   Accounting Information-Companies

1	2	3	4	5	6	7
Country and type of company (if necessary)	Requirement to keep accounting records	Accounting records meet a, b, c, d*	Requirement to prepare financial statements	Requirement to file financial statements with a Governmental Authority and/or file a requisite tax return	Requirement to have financial statements audited	Retention period for accounting records
Saint Kitts and Nevis *Nevis Limited Liability Company Ordinance*	Yes, in respect of those LLCs which carry on financial services business.	Yes, in respect of those LLCs which carry on financial services business.	Yes, in respect of those LLCs which carry on financial services business.	Yes, in respect of those LLCs which carry on financial services business.	Yes, in respect of those LLCs which carry on financial services business.	5 years under anti-money laundering regulations.
Saint Lucia *Companies Act*	Yes	Yes	Yes	Yes	Yes, for public companies.	7 years
Saint Lucia *International Business Companies Act*	Yes	Yes: a & b And all a, b, c & d when engaged in a regulated activity.	No, unless engaged in a regulated activity.	No, unless engaged in a regulated activity.	No, unless engaged in a regulated activity.	7 years
Saint Vincent and the Grenadines *Companies Act*	Yes	Yes	Yes	Yes	Yes for public and non-profit companies.	7 years in accordance with the Proceeds of Crime Money Laundering Prevention Act.
Saint Vincent and the Grenadines *International Business Companies*	Yes	Yes: a & b And all a, b, c & d when engaged in a regulated activity.	No, unless engaged in a regulated activity.	No, unless engaged in a regulated activity.	No, unless engaged in a regulated activity.	7years in accordance with the Proceeds of Crime Money Laundering Prevention Act.
Samoa *Domestic companies*	Yes	Yes	Yes	Yes, companies that are subject to income tax are required to lodge a return.	Yes, unless in the case of a private company where the members resolve otherwise.	7/12 years
Samoa *International companies*	No, required to keep such accounts and records as the directors consider necessary or desirable.	No, except for international financial institutions and Segregated Fund International Companies.	No	No	No	7 years
San Marino	Yes	Yes	Yes	Yes	No, unless special legislation requirements, such as for the Central Bank.	5 years

Table D.6   Accounting Information-Companies

1	2	3	4	5	6	7
Country and type of company (if necessary)	Requirement to keep accounting records	Accounting records meet a, b, c, d*	Requirement to prepare financial statements	Requirement to file financial statements with a Governmental Authority and/or file a requisite tax return	Requirement to have financial statements audited	Retention period for accounting records
Seychelles *Companies Act*	Yes	Yes	Yes	Yes	No, except for regulated activities.	7 years
Seychelles *International Business Companies Act*	Yes	Yes: a & b	No	No	No	6 years
Singapore	Yes	Yes	Yes	Yes, where carrying on business in Singapore or subject to Singapore income tax.	Yes, with an exception for dormant and small companies.	7 years
Slovak Republic	Yes	Yes: a, b & c	Yes	Yes	Yes, depending on the size of a company.	5 years (10 years for financial statements and annual reports).
South Africa	Yes	Yes	Yes	Public companies (but not close corporations) must file financial statements for regulatory purposes. All companies must file tax returns.	Yes, for public companies	5 years
Spain	Yes	Yes	Yes	Yes. An abridged version allowed for smaller entities.	Yes, where exceeds the limit to provide abridged accounts.	6 years
Sweden	Yes	Yes	Yes	Yes	Yes	10 years
Switzerland	Yes	Yes: a, c & d	Yes	Yes	Yes for companies limited by share.s	10 years
Turkey	Yes	Yes	Yes	Yes	Yes	5 years
Turks and Caicos Islands	Yes	Yes: a, b & d And all a, b c & d when engaged in a regulated activity.	No, unless engaged in a regulated activity.	No, unless engaged in a regulated activity.	No, unless engaged in a regulated activity.	10 years

Table D.6   Accounting Information-Companies

1	2	3	4	5	6	7
Country and type of company (if necessary)	Requirement to keep accounting records	Accounting records meet a, b, c, d*	Requirement to prepare financial statements	Requirement to file financial statements with a Governmental Authority and/or file a requisite tax return	Requirement to have financial statements audited	Retention period for accounting records
United Arab Emirates	Yes	Federal companies: Yes. DIFC Companies: a,b,c	Yes	Yes, all companies are required to file financial statements with a government authority.	Yes	Federal companies: no requirement. DIFC companies:10 years.
United Kingdom	Yes	Yes	Yes	Yes, all companies that are liable to tax must file returns. All limited companies are required to file accounts with the Registrar of Companies.	Yes, except for dormant companies and small companies.	6 years
United States	Yes	Yes	Yes, for corporations exceeding a certain size.	Yes. All domestic corporations must file a return of income.	No	Yes, so long as the contents thereof may become material in the administration of any internal revenue law. Ordinarily this period would be a minimum of three years and frequently is indefinitely longer.
United States Virgin Islands	Yes	a, c & d (b: the company's position can only be determined with reasonable accuracy at the end of a tax period).	Unclear	Domestic companies must file an annual tax return. However, unless an exempt company earns income from a United States or USVI source, or income that is effectively connected with a trade or business in one of those jurisdictions, it does not have to file an income tax return.	International insurance companies.	Yes, so long as the contents thereof may become material in the administration of any internal revenue law. Ordinarily this period would be a minimum of three years and frequently is indefinitely longer.

Table D.6   Accounting Information-Companies

1	2	3	4	5	6	7
Country and type of company (if necessary)	Requirement to keep accounting records	Accounting records meet a, b, c, d*	Requirement to prepare financial statements	Requirement to file financial statements with a Governmental Authority and/or file a requisite tax return	Requirement to have financial statements audited	Retention period for accounting records
Uruguay	Yes	Yes	Yes	Yes, all companies carrying on business activities except free trade zone companies must file tax returns. Companies of a certain size must file accounts with the National Audit Office.	Yes for banks, listed companies and companies with debts in excess of certain limits.	20 years
Vanuatu *Local and exempt companies*	Yes	Yes	Yes	Yes, financial statements but no tax return.	Yes, depending on the economic size of a company.	5 years
Vanuatu *International companies*	Yes	Yes: b	No	No	No	No

Table D.7
Accounting Information-Trusts

Explanation of columns 2 through 6

Column 2 lists the countries that have a domestic trust law requirement to keep accounting records. **Column 3** sets out the type of records that are required to be kept pursuant to domestic trust laws. **Columns 4** and **5** examine requirements to keep accounting records pursuant to other laws (such as taxation or anti-money laundering requirements). **Column 6** records the relevant retention period.

Table D.7   Accounting Information-Trusts

1	2	3	4	5	6	7
Country and type of trust (if necessary)	**Required to keep accounting records pursuant to domestic trust law**	**Type of accounting records kept under domestic trust law**	**Required for resident trustee to keep accounting records based on law other than trust law**	**Type of accounting records required to be kept under law other than trust law**	**Retention period for accounting records**	**Notes**
Anguilla	Yes	'The trustee shall keep accurate accounts of his trusteeship'.	No	No	7 years	Mutual funds formed as unit trusts must prepare audited financial statements.
Antigua and Barbuda	No information.	No information.	No information.	No information.	No information.	
Argentina	No	N/A	Yes	Inventories, balance sheets, profit and loss accounts.	10 years	
Australia	Yes	Sufficient to be able to properly account to the beneficiaries.	Yes, taxation law where subject to taxation or required to lodge a return.	Sufficient to explain the amount of gross income, deductions, credits or other amounts required to be shown in any return.	5 years	
The Bahamas	Yes	For all trusts-common law duty. Purpose Trusts-Documents sufficient to show the trust's true financial position for each financial year together with details of all applications of principle and income during that financial year.	Yes. Professional trustees, which must be licensed, must comply with anti-money laundering requirements and keep "transaction records".	Anti-money laundering-transaction records.	12 years to satisfy the common law obligation. For anti-money laundering purposes, the basic retention period for transaction records in the case of professional trustees is 5 years.	

Table D.7   Accounting Information-Trusts

1	2	3	4	5	6	7
Country and type of trust (if necessary)	Required to keep accounting records pursuant to domestic trust law	Type of accounting records kept under domestic trust law	Required for resident trustee to keep accounting records based on law other than trust law	Type of accounting records required to be kept under law other than trust law	Retention period for accounting records	Notes
Bahrain *Financial Trust*	Yes	The trustee is required to maintain records and account-books, and record, in a regular and orderly manner, all transactions and works relating to the trust. These must be kept separate from the records of any other business carried out by the trustee. The trust accounts must be audited, unless the trust instrument or a subsequent agreement or the nature of dealing with the trust property require otherwise.	No	N/A.	No	
Barbados	Yes	Trustee of a trust shall keep accurate accounts and records of his trusteeship.*	Yes, pursuant to taxation law where subject to taxation or required to lodge a return. Trustees of an international non-charitable purpose trust are also required to retain documents that reflect the true financial position of the trust.	Sufficient to explain the amount of gross income, deductions, credits or other amounts required to be shown in any return.	Indefinite, however permission can be granted after 9 years to dispose of certain records. When a trust is not formed under a Barbadian law, the retention is not required unless the trust is resident.	*A trust that carries on business is required to prepare audited financial statements and submit them to the Inland Revenue Dept.

Table D.7 Accounting Information-Trusts

1	2	3	4	5	6	7
Country and type of trust (if necessary)	Required to keep accounting records pursuant to domestic trust law	Type of accounting records kept under domestic trust law	Required for resident trustee to keep accounting records based on law other than trust law	Type of accounting records required to be kept under law other than trust law	Retention period for accounting records	Notes
Belize	Yes	Trustee of a trust shall keep accurate accounts and records of his trusteeship. Public Unit Trusts must keep, have audited and file annual accounts prepared in accordance with generally accepted accounting and auditing standards.	Yes, taxation law where subject to taxation or required to lodge a return.	Sufficient to explain the amount of gross income, deductions, credits or other amounts required to be shown in any return.	6 years	
Bermuda	Yes	Financial records must be maintained so as to permit a thorough and satisfactory supervisory review and to permit the performance of trust audits as pre-arranged. Trustees are also subject to a common law duty to maintain accounting records.	No	No	No	Trustees of unit trusts which are regulated as investment funds are required to prepare financial statements and to file an annual audit with the Regulator.
British Virgin Islands	Yes	Common law duty to maintain accounting records for the trust.	No	N/A	5 years	Public mutual funds formed as unit trusts and licensed under the Mutual Funds Act must produce annual audited accounts.
Brunei	No	No requirement.	No information.	No information.	No information.	

Table D.7   Accounting Information-Trusts

1	2	3	4	5	6	7
Country and type of trust (if necessary)	**Required to keep accounting records pursuant to domestic trust law**	**Type of accounting records kept under domestic trust law**	**Required for resident trustee to keep accounting records based on law other than trust law**	**Type of accounting records required to be kept under law other than trust law**	**Retention period for accounting records**	**Notes**
Canada	Yes	Sufficient to be able to properly account to the beneficiaries.	Yes, taxation law where subject to taxation or required to lodge a return.	Sufficient to explain the amount of gross income, deductions, credits or other amounts required to be shown in any return.	6 years	
Cayman Islands	Yes	Special Trusts-Alternatives Regime trusts: Documentary records of the trust property, settlements and distributions. Other trusts: Common law requirements apply.	Yes, any entity conducting relevant financial business, including trustees, must comply with anti-money laundering record keeping obligations.	Details of personal identity, including the names and addresses, of the customer, the beneficial owner of the account or product and any counter party. Transactional records including where relevant the nature of securities / investments; valuation and prices; memoranda of purchase and sale; source and volume of funds; destination of funds; memoranda of instruction and authority; book entries; custody of title documentation; the nature of the transaction; the date of the transaction and the form in which funds are paid out.	As required by trust law. Anti-money laundering laws also impose a 5 year retention period for relevant records.	Mutual funds formed as unit trusts under the Mutual Funds Law must prepare audited financial statements.

Table D.7   Accounting Information-Trusts

1	2	3	4	5	6	7
Country and type of trust (if necessary)	Required to keep accounting records pursuant to domestic trust law	Type of accounting records kept under domestic trust law	Required for resident trustee to keep accounting records based on law other than trust law	Type of accounting records required to be kept under law other than trust law	Retention period for accounting records	Notes
China	Yes	Records of the management of a trust.	Yes, a tax law.	Account books, account vouchers, financial reports and original vouchers.	10 years	
Cook Islands *Domestic trusts*	No	No	Yes, for tax purposes.	Sufficient records for assessable income and allowable deductions to be readily ascertained.	5 years (6 years for anti-money laundering purposes).	
Cook Islands *International trusts*	No	No	No	No	6 years for anti-money laundering purposes.	
Costa Rica	Yes	In accordance with requirements of the Commercial Code.	Yes, taxation law where subject to taxation or required to lodge a return.	Sufficient to explain the amount of gross income, deductions, credits or other amounts required to be shown in any return.	4 years	
Cyprus	Yes	A general duty to maintain accounting records for the trust.	No	No	7 years	International Unit Trust Schemes are required to prepare annual and semi-annual accounts.
Dominica	No	No	No	No	No	
Gibraltar	Yes	Sufficient to be able to properly account to the beneficiaries.	Yes, taxation law where subject to taxation or required to lodge a return.	Sufficient to explain the amount of gross income, deductions, credits or other amounts required to be shown in any return.	6 years	

Table D.7   Accounting Information-Trusts

1	2	3	4	5	6	7
Country and type of trust (if necessary)	Required to keep accounting records pursuant to domestic trust law	Type of accounting records kept under domestic trust law	Required for resident trustee to keep accounting records based on law other than trust law	Type of accounting records required to be kept under law other than trust law	Retention period for accounting records	Notes
Grenada *International trusts*	Yes	Trustees must keep such documents as are necessary to show the true financial position at the end of the trust's financial year together with details of the application of principal and income during the year.	No	No	7 years	
Guatemala	Yes	No requirement.	Yes, for tax purposes.	Must maintain at least one cash revenue and expenditure journal and one inventory book to record assets and debts.	5 years	
Guernsey	Yes	Full and accurate accounts and records of trusteeship.	Yes, for tax purposes where the trustees receive business income or income from the letting of property subject to Guernsey tax. Unit trusts are also required to submit reports and financial statements to the regulator.	For tax purposes detailed records have to be maintained of income and expenditure and underlying documentation has to be retained. For Unit trusts: annual accounts in accordance with generally accepted accounting principles.	6 years, but, for income tax purposes, with effect from 1 January 2007, trustees that carry on a business or receive income from the letting of property must retain their records for 6 years after the end of the year in which the relevant income tax return was submitted.	Trust service providers must keep and preserve appropriate records of trust business.
Hong Kong, China	Yes	Sufficient records to be able to properly account to the beneficiaries.	Yes, under taxation law if the trustee is chargeable to profit tax thereunder.	Sufficient records of income and expenditure to enable the profits to be readily ascertained.	7 years	For those registered as trust companies, the Companies Ordinance applied.

Table D.7   Accounting Information-Trusts

1	2	3	4	5	6	7
Country and type of trust (if necessary)	Required to keep accounting records pursuant to domestic trust law	Type of accounting records kept under domestic trust law	Required for resident trustee to keep accounting records based on law other than trust law	Type of accounting records required to be kept under law other than trust law	Retention period for accounting records	Notes
Ireland	Yes	Sufficient to show and explain all of the trust's transactions.	Yes, tax law.	Same as for other taxpayers - money spent and received/ purchases and sales/ assets and liabilities. Unit trusts must prepare annual audited accounts.	6 years	
Isle of Man	Yes	Sufficient to be able to properly account to beneficiaries.	Yes, taxation law where subject to taxation or required to lodge a return.	Sufficient to explain the amount of gross income, deductions, credits or other amounts required to be shown in any return.	No*	*Fiduciary service providers are required to keep and preserve appropriate records of trust business.
Japan	Yes	Sufficient to show and explain all the trust's transactions and calculations.	Yes, tax laws.	Those required under tax laws.	7 years	
Jersey	Yes	Full and accurate accounts and records of trusteeship.	Yes, taxation law where subject to taxation or required to lodge a return. Unit trusts are also required to submit reports and financial statements to the financial regulator.	Sufficient to explain the amount of gross income, deductions, credits or other amounts required to be shown in any return. For unit trusts, annual accounts in accordance with generally accepted accounting principles.	5 years	Trust service providers must keep and preserve appropriate records of trust business.
Korea	Yes	Management and financial results.	No	N/A	No	

Table D.7   Accounting Information-Trusts

1	2	3	4	5	6	7
Country and type of trust (if necessary)	**Required to keep accounting records pursuant to domestic trust law**	**Type of accounting records kept under domestic trust law**	**Required for resident trustee to keep accounting records based on law other than trust law**	**Type of accounting records required to be kept under law other than trust law**	**Retention period for accounting records**	**Notes**
Liechtenstein	Yes	Trustee must maintain an 'inventory of assets' to be revised and updated annually. Trustee must further be in position to inform on status of trusteeship at any time. Licensed trustee of certain business trusts must file declaration confirming that statement of assets and liabilities is available.	No	No	No	
Macao, China	No	No	No	No	No	Accounting records required for a trust management company.
Malaysia	Yes	No information.	Yes (tax purposes).	No information.	7 years	
Malta	Yes	Accurate accounting records and records of trusteeship in accordance with Malta's Trust legislation.	Yes, an anti-money laundering law.	Anti-money laundering rules require retention of "Record containing details relating to all transactions carried out by that person in the course of an established business relationship".	5 years	

Table D.7   Accounting Information-Trusts

1	2	3	4	5	6	7
Country and type of trust (if necessary)	Required to keep accounting records pursuant to domestic trust law	Type of accounting records kept under domestic trust law	Required for resident trustee to keep accounting records based on law other than trust law	Type of accounting records required to be kept under law other than trust law	Retention period for accounting records	Notes
Mauritius	Yes	Depends on the type of activities carried on by the trust.	A qualified trustee must keep accounting records for anti-money laundering purposes.	Records of transactions conducted in the course of business relationship.	7 years	Public Mutual Funds and a trust holding a Category 1 Global Business License must submit annual audited accounts.
Mexico	Yes	Sufficient to be able to properly account to beneficiaries.	Yes, taxation law where subject to taxation or required to lodge a return.	Sufficient to explain the amount of gross income, deductions, credits or other amounts required to be shown in any return.	5 years	
Monaco *Trusts formed under foreign laws*	No	No	No	No	No	
Montserrat	Yes	Accounting records sufficient to show the true financial position of a trust.	No	No	6 years	Mutual funds formed as unit trusts must file financial statements.
Nauru	Yes	No	No	No	No	
New Zealand	Yes	Sufficient to be able to properly account to beneficiaries.	Yes, taxation law where subject to taxation or required to lodge a return.	Sufficient to explain the amount of gross income, deductions, credits or other amounts required to be shown in any return.	7 years	
Niue	Yes	Accurate accounts and records of trusteeship.	Yes, trustees other than those of tax exempt trusts are required to keep records according to the tax ordinance.	Sufficient records to allow the assessable income and allowable deductions to be readily ascertained.	7 years	

Table D.7   Accounting Information-Trusts

1	2	3	4	5	6	7
Country and type of trust (if necessary)	Required to keep accounting records pursuant to domestic trust law	Type of accounting records kept under domestic trust law	Required for resident trustee to keep accounting records based on law other than trust law	Type of accounting records required to be kept under law other than trust law	Retention period for accounting records	Notes
Panama	Yes	Sufficient to be able to properly account to beneficiaries.	Yes, taxation law where subject to taxation or required to lodge a return. Also the Commercial Code if a merchant.	Sufficient to explain the amount of gross income, deductions, credits or other amounts required to be shown in any return.	5 years	
Philippines	Yes	Maintain books and records.	Yes, tax law.	Similar to a company.	3 years	
Saint Kitts and Nevis *Trusts Act*	Yes	Accounting records sufficient to show and explain transactions and are such as to disclose with reasonable accuracy at any time the financial position of a trust.	No	No	No	
Saint Kitts and Nevis *Nevis International Exempt Trusts Ordinance*	No	No	Yes	Accounting records showing a true and fair view of the state of affairs for the financial year.	5 years under anti-money laundering regulations.	Trust businesses which carry on financial services business are required to prepare financial statements, audited by an independent auditor.
Saint Lucia *International Trust*	No	No	No	No	No	Mutual funds formed as unit trusts must file audited financial statements.
Saint Lucia *Other local trusts*	No	No	Yes, for tax purposes. Unit trusts are required to file accounts with the financial services regulator.	Maintain sufficient records and accounts to enable correct tax assessment.	7 years	

Table D.7   Accounting Information-Trusts

1	2	3	4	5	6	7
Country and type of trust (if necessary)	Required to keep accounting records pursuant to domestic trust law	Type of accounting records kept under domestic trust law	Required for resident trustee to keep accounting records based on law other than trust law	Type of accounting records required to be kept under law other than trust law	Retention period for accounting records	Notes
Saint Vincent and the Grenadines	Yes	Books and records necessary to show the true financial position of a trust.	Yes, the Registered Agent and Trustee Licensing Act.	Books and records that accurately reflect the business of each trust.	7 years	Public mutual funds formed as unit trusts must produce annual audited accounts. Private and accredited mutual funds must file annual accounts.
Samoa	Yes	Sufficient to be able to properly account to beneficiaries.	Yes, taxation law where subject to taxation or required to lodge a return.	Sufficient to explain the amount of gross income, deductions, credits or other amounts required to be shown in any return.	7 years under anti-money laundering legislation	
San Marino	Yes	Sufficient to be able to properly account to beneficiaries.	Yes, for a tax law.	Sufficient to be able to properly account to beneficiaries.	5 years	
Seychelles	Yes	Keep strict and accurate accounts and records of trusteeship.	Yes, the International Corporate Service Provider Act.	Maintain accounts which separately show each client's funds.	7 years	
Singapore	Yes	Sufficient to be able to properly account to beneficiaries. Licensed trust companies are required to account for their trusts' financial positions and the transactions entered on behalf of the trusts.	Yes, tax law where relevant. Laws relating to unit trusts, business trusts and charitable trusts also contain requirements to keep records.	Sufficient to explain the amount of gross income, deductions, credits or other amounts required to be shown in any return.	6/7 years	

Table D.7   Accounting Information-Trusts

1	2	3	4	5	6	7
Country and type of trust (if necessary)	Required to keep accounting records pursuant to domestic trust law	Type of accounting records kept under domestic trust law	Required for resident trustee to keep accounting records based on law other than trust law	Type of accounting records required to be kept under law other than trust law	Retention period for accounting records	Notes
South Africa	Yes	Necessary to fairly represent the trust's state of affairs and business and to explain its transactions and financial position. Annual statements.	Yes, for tax purposes.	Necessary to fairly represent the trust's state of affairs and business and to explain its transactions and financial position. Annual statements.	No statutory retention period.	
Turks and Caicos Islands	No	No	Yes, the Trustee (Licensing) Ordinance.	Records must be sufficient to give a full account of the trust assets.	10 years	Public mutual funds formed as licensed unit trusts must produce annual audited accounts.
United Arab Emirates	Yes	Trustee is required to keep accurate accounts and records of his trusteeship. Required documents include audited financial statements, profit and loss statement and title of assets held in trust.	No	No	During the life of the trust and for 6 years following dissolution.	The DIFC Trust law requires trustees to maintain accounts during their tenure. A trust service provider must prepare proper accounts at appropriately regular intervals on the trusts and underlying companies administered for clients. In any case, the trust service provider's books and records must be sufficient to allow the recreation of the transactions of the business and its clients and to demonstrate what assets are due to each client and what liabilities are attributable to each client.

Table D.7   Accounting Information-Trusts

1	2	3	4	5	6	7
Country and type of trust (if necessary)	Required to keep accounting records pursuant to domestic trust law	Type of accounting records kept under domestic trust law	Required for resident trustee to keep accounting records based on law other than trust law	Type of accounting records required to be kept under law other than trust law	Retention period for accounting records	Notes
United Kingdom	Yes	Sufficient to show and explain all the trust's transactions.	Yes, for taxation.	Sufficient to enable a correct and complete tax return to be made.	For tax purposes, 5 years if trustees are trading or letting property; otherwise 22 months.	
United States	Yes	Sufficient to be able to properly account to beneficiaries.	Yes, taxation law where a return is required to be filed. (Response limited to federal tax law: other laws may apply).	Sufficient to explain the amount of gross income, deductions, credits or other amounts required to be shown in any return.	Yes, so long as the contents thereof may become material in the administration of any internal revenue law. Ordinarily this period would be a minimum of three years and frequently is indefinitely longer.	
United States Virgin Islands	Yes	Sufficient to be able to properly account to beneficiaries.	Yes, taxation law where subject to taxation or required to lodge a return.	Sufficient to explain the amount of gross income, deductions, credits or other amounts required to be shown in any return.	Yes, so long as the contents thereof may become material in the administration of any internal revenue law. Ordinarily this period would be a minimum of three years and frequently is indefinitely longer.	
Uruguay	Yes	Inventory and assets and liabilities constituting the property of a trust.	Yes, where trust is taxable.	Ledger, inventory book and copies of all documents.	20 years if a trust carries out a business activity.	

Table D.7   Accounting Information-Trusts

1	2	3	4	5	6	7
Country and type of trust (if necessary)	Required to keep accounting records pursuant to domestic trust law	Type of accounting records kept under domestic trust law	Required for resident trustee to keep accounting records based on law other than trust law	Type of accounting records required to be kept under law other than trust law	Retention period for accounting records	Notes
Vanuatu	Yes	Depending on the complexity of a trust but must be sufficiently detailed to fairly disclose the financial situation.	No	No	6 years for anti-money laundering purposes.	

Table D.8
Accounting Information-Partnerships

Explanation of columns 2 through 4

This table dealing with partnerships sets out whether there is a requirement to keep accounting records **(column 2)**, the type of accounting records required to be kept **(column 3)** and the period of time such records must be retained **(column 4)**.

Table D.8   Accounting Information-Partnerships

1	2	3	4	5
Country and type of partnership (if necessary)	Requirement to keep accounting records for partnerships formed under domestic law	Type of accounting records kept for partnerships formed under domestic law	Retention period for accounting records	Notes
Anguilla	Yes, for local general partnerships, but no, for limited partnerships.	Sufficient to render true accounts and full information of all things affecting the partnership to any partner or his agents. Sufficient to render true accounts and full information of all things affecting the partnership to any partner or his agents.	6 years	If a limited partnership engaged in an activity requiring a license, audited financial statements required.
Argentina	Yes	A journal and an inventory and financial statements books as well as subsidiary books. The transactions should be recorded in chronological order in the journal. The inventory and financial statements book should contain itemized annual financial statements.	10 years	
Aruba	Yes	Explain transactions, enable a financial position to be determined, and include underlying documentation.	10 years	
Australia	Yes	To meet requirements of partnership and sufficient to explain the amount of gross income, deductions, credits or other amounts required to be shown in any return.	5 years	
Austria	Yes	Tax law requires all records necessary for the determination of the tax liability. The commercial law further requires double entry book keeping; small partnerships may use cash accounting method.	7 years	
The Bahamas	Yes	Common law duty to account. In addition licensed service providers must maintain transaction records in relation to activities of partnerships performed by them.	5 years for transaction records for anti-money laundering.	
Bahrain	Yes	Proper books of account and records sufficient to enable true financial position of a partnership to be determined; balance sheet and profit and loss statement.	10 year (5 years for records and supporting materials).	

Table D.8 Accounting Information-Partnerships

1	2	3	4	5
Country and type of partnership (if necessary)	**Requirement to keep accounting records for partnerships formed under domestic law**	**Type of accounting records kept for partnerships formed under domestic law**	**Retention period for accounting records**	**Notes**
Barbados	Yes	To meet requirements of partnership and sufficient to explain the amount of gross income, deductions, credits or other amounts required to be shown in any return.	Indefinite; however permission can be granted after 9 years to dispose of certain records.	
Belgium	Yes	To meet requirements of partnership and sufficient to explain the amount of gross income, deductions, credits or other amounts required to be shown in any return.	10 years	
Belize	Yes	To meet requirements of partnership and sufficient to explain the amount of gross income, deductions, credits or other amounts required to be shown in any return.	5-6 years	
Bermuda	Yes	For all partnerships, records sufficient to render true accounts and full information of all things affecting the partnership to any partner or his legal representative. Specific requirements for exempted partnerships include records of account with respect to (i) assets, liabilities and capital, (ii) cash receipts and disbursements, iii) purchases and sales, and iv) income costs and expenses. Exempted partnerships are required to prepare financial statements in accordance with generally accepted accounting principles but not file with governmental authority. Additional records are required for a licensed financial provider.	No	There is no express duty to keep accounting records for unlicensed entities. There is a duty imposed on partners under the Partnership Act to render accounts to any partner.
British Virgin Islands	Yes	Partners are bound to render true accounts and full information of all things affecting the partnership to any partner or his agents.	5 years	Audited financial statements required if engaged in an activity requiring a license.

Table D.8   Accounting Information-Partnerships

1	2	3	4	5
Country and type of partnership (if necessary)	Requirement to keep accounting records for partnerships formed under domestic law	Type of accounting records kept for partnerships formed under domestic law	Retention period for accounting records	Notes
Brunei *International Partnerships*	Yes	Such accounts and records as are sufficient to show and explain an international partnership's transactions and to disclose with reasonable accuracy at any time the financial position of the partnership at that time.	No information.	No information.
Canada	Yes	To meet requirements of partnership and sufficient to explain the amount of gross income, deductions, credits or other amounts required to be shown in any return.	6 years	
Cayman Islands	Yes	Partners are bound to render true accounts and full information of all things affecting the partnership to any partner or his agents.	5 years for anti-money laundering purposes. Otherwise depends on the nature of partnership activities.	Mutual funds formed as partnerships must prepare audited financial statements.
China	Yes	Account books, account vouchers, financial reports and original vouchers.	10 years	
Cook Islands	Yes	Depends on the type of business a partnership engages in.	5 years	
Costa Rica	Yes	To meet requirements of partnership and sufficient to explain the amount of gross income, deductions, credits or other amounts required to be shown in any return.	4 years	
Cyprus	Yes	Books or accounts as are necessary to exhibit or explain their transactions and financial position in their trade, business, or profession.	7 years	
Denmark	Yes	To meet requirements of partnership and sufficient to explain the amount of gross income, deductions, credits or other amounts required to be shown in any return.	5 years	
Dominica	No information.	No information.	No information.	

Table D.8   Accounting Information-Partnerships

1	2	3	4	5
Country and type of partnership (if necessary)	**Requirement to keep accounting records for partnerships formed under domestic law**	**Type of accounting records kept for partnerships formed under domestic law**	**Retention period for accounting records**	**Notes**
Finland	Yes	All business transactions must be presented in order of recording and in systematic order. It must be possible at all times to control the completeness of the accounting entry posting and form an overall picture of the events, balance and result of the business activity. For every business transaction there must be a voucher. An annual report must be drawn up that gives a true and fair view of the partnerships' assets, liabilities and equity, financial position and results for the year.	10 years	
Germany	Yes	Accounting records necessary to permit the calculation of taxable income.	10 years	The Commercial Code imposes additional requirements for commercial partnerships (general and limited partnership).
Gibraltar	Yes	To meet requirements of partnership and sufficient to explain the amount of gross income, deductions, credits or other amounts required to be shown in any return.	6 years	
Guatemala	Yes	Financial statements, with exceptions for small businesses.	5 years	
Guernsey *General partnerships*	Yes	Partners must render true accounts and full information on all things affecting the partnership to any partner or his personal representative. In addition, if the partners are in receipt of income from a business, or from the letting of property, with effect from 1 January 2007 new legislation requires detailed records to be maintained of income and expenditure and underlying documentation has to be retained.	6 years but, for income tax purposes, with effect from 1 January 2007, for partnerships that carry on a business or receive income from the letting of property, the partners must retain their records for 6 years after the end of the year in which the relevant income tax return was submitted.	

Table D.8   Accounting Information-Partnerships

1	2	3	4	5
Country and type of partnership (if necessary)	**Requirement to keep accounting records for partnerships formed under domestic law**	**Type of accounting records kept for partnerships formed under domestic law**	**Retention period for accounting records**	**Notes**
Guernsey *Limited partnerships*	Yes	Records must be sufficient to show and explain transactions, to disclose the financial position, and to ensure that its balance sheet and profit and loss account are prepared properly. In addition, if the partners are in receipt of income from a business, or from the letting of property, with effect from 1 January 2007 new legislation requires detailed records to be maintained of income and expenditure and underlying documentation has to be retained.	6 years, but, for income tax purposes, with effect from 1 January 2007, for partnerships that carry on a business or receive income from the letting of property, the partners must retain their records for 6 years after the end of the year in which the relevant income tax return was submitted.	Financial statements for limited partnerships structured as open or closed-ended collective investment funds must be provided to the Guernsey Financial Services Commission.
Hong Kong, China	Yes	Same as for companies.	7 years	
Iceland	Yes	Accounts must provide such information on operations and the asset balance as demanded by owners, creditors and public bodies and is necessary to assess revenue and expenditure, assets and liabilities. Annual accounts must be drawn up once a year.	7 years	
Ireland	Yes	Same as those for other taxpayers carrying on business.	6 years	Annual audited accounts required for Investment Limited Partnership.
Isle of Man	Yes	Sufficient to disclose a true and fair view of a partnership's financial state of affairs in accordance with current accounting practices applicable to partnerships.	No	
Italy	Yes, where carrying on a business.	Same as those for other taxpayers carrying on business.	10 years	

Table D.8   Accounting Information-Partnerships

1	2	3	4	5
Country and type of partnership (if necessary)	Requirement to keep accounting records for partnerships formed under domestic law	Type of accounting records kept for partnerships formed under domestic law	Retention period for accounting records	Notes
Jersey	Yes	To meet requirements of partnership and sufficient to explain the amount of gross income, deductions, credits or other amounts required to be shown in any return. In respect of general partnerships: to meet requirements of partnership and sufficient to explain the amount of gross income, deductions, credits or other amounts required to be shown in any return. For limited partnerships: sufficient to show and explain transactions and to disclose with reasonable accuracy the financial position at any time. For limited liability partnerships: to maintain proper accounting records.	10 years for Limited Liability Partnerships.	
Liechtenstein	Yes	Opening balance sheet; account showing all assets and liabilities at the end of each financial year; annual report consisting of a balance sheet and profit and loss statement accompanied by notes where necessary.	10 years	Accounting rules applicable to companies apply to unlimited and limited partnerships where all partners with unlimited liability are companies.
Luxembourg	Yes	Sufficient to enable a partnership's financial position to be established at least at the end of the business period and to enable financial statements to be prepared.	10 years	
Malaysia	No information.	No information.	7 years other than Labuan which has no specified period.	
Malta	Yes	Detailed rules apply under company, commercial as well as tax laws.	10 years	There are additional and more specific rules for limited partnerships that are used as collective investment funds and for certain other partnerships.
Marshall Islands	Yes	Information on the partnership's financial condition and, when applicable, copies of the partnership's income tax returns, for each year.	No	

Table D.8   Accounting Information-Partnerships

1	2	3	4	5
Country and type of partnership (if necessary)	Requirement to keep accounting records for partnerships formed under domestic law	Type of accounting records kept for partnerships formed under domestic law	Retention period for accounting records	Notes
Mauritius	Yes	Books and records enabling the Commissioner to ascertain the gross income and allowable deductions.	5 years	Audited financial statements required for a partnership engaged in financial services sector.
Mexico	Yes	To meet requirements of partnership and sufficient to explain the amount of gross income, deductions, credits or other amounts required to be shown in any return.	5 years	
Montserrat	Yes	No information.	6 years	
Nauru	Yes	Not specified.	No	
Netherlands	Yes	Books and records and all facts pertaining to business shall be kept and retained in such a way that they clearly show at any moment in time, a partnerships' rights and obligations, as well as any data which are otherwise of importance to the levying of taxes.	7 years	
Netherlands Antilles	Yes	Financial statements.	10 years	
New Zealand	Yes	To meet requirements of partnership and sufficient to explain the amount of gross income, deductions, credits or other amounts required to be shown in any return.	7 years	
Niue	Yes	True accounts and full information.	7 years	
Norway	Yes	Financial statements.	3, 5 or 10 years; depending on type of document.	
Panama	Yes	Same as for companies.	5 years	
Philippines	Yes	Same as for companies.	3 years	
Poland	Yes, simplified reporting admitted for a certain type of partnership.	Same as for companies.	Permanently for approved financial statements; 5 years for other files.	

Table D.8   Accounting Information-Partnerships

1	2	3	4	5
Country and type of partnership (if necessary)	**Requirement to keep accounting records for partnerships formed under domestic law**	**Type of accounting records kept for partnerships formed under domestic law**	**Retention period for accounting records**	**Notes**
Russian Federation	Yes	The main aim of accounting records is to form full and accurate information on the activity of an enterprise and its assets. The accounting records must also include sufficient information to determine the taxable income.	4 years	
Saint Kitts and Nevis *Limited partnerships (applicable only in Saint Kitts)*	Yes	Accounting records sufficient to show and explain their transactions in respect of a limited partnership and are such as to disclose with reasonable accuracy at any time the financial position of the limited partnership.	No	Limited partnership carrying out activities requiring a license must file annual audited accounts. The Consumption Tax Act requires persons engaged in business activities to keep records of their gross revenue.
Saint Lucia	Yes	Must render true accounts and full information of all things affecting a partnership.	No	Partners subject to tax must satisfy the auditing and filing requirements of the Income Tax Act.
Saint Vincent and the Grenadines	Yes	Must render true accounts and full information of all things affecting a partnership to any partner or his legal representative.	6 years	Partnerships operate only locally.
Samoa *Domestic partnership*	Yes	To meet requirements of a partnership and sufficient to explain the amount of gross income, deductions, credits or other amounts required to be shown in any return.	12 years	
Samoa *International and limited partnerships*	Yes	Sufficient to allow the general partner to account to other partners.	7 years	
San Marino	Yes	A day and a cash book, a book inventory and a book of depreciable assets and original copies of the correspondence and invoices received as well as copies of the correspondence and invoices sent. A certain type of partnership is subject to all accounting requirements of a company.	5 years	
Seychelles	Yes	Accounting records equivalent to those required to be kept by companies.	No	

Table D.8   Accounting Information-Partnerships

1	2	3	4	5
Country and type of partnership (if necessary)	Requirement to keep accounting records for partnerships formed under domestic law	Type of accounting records kept for partnerships formed under domestic law	Retention period for accounting records	Notes
Singapore	Yes	The Partnership Act requires records sufficient to render true accounts and full information of all things affecting the partnership to any partner. Whereas the Limited Liability Partnership Act requires records sufficient to explain the transactions and financial position of a limited partnership and enable profit and loss and balance sheets to be prepared which give a true and fair view.	7 years	
South Africa	Yes, common law rights and obligations.	Each partner is obliged to render an account of his administration of the partnership business to other partners. A formal partnership account must be rendered annually or at such times which accord with usual business usage. An account must also be rendered upon dissolution of the partnership. The Income Tax Law requires that accounts include all information that is necessary to determine the taxable income for the partners.	No statutory requirements.	
Sweden	Yes	All business transactions must be presented in order of recording and in systematic order. It must be possible at all times to control the completeness of the accounting entry posting and form an overall picture of the events, balance and result of the business activity. For every business transaction there must be a voucher. For larger partnerships and for those where at least one of the partners is a legal person an annual report must be drawn up that gives a true and fair view of the partnership's assets, liabilities and equity, financial position and results for the year.	10 years	

Table D.8 Accounting Information-Partnerships

1	2	3	4	5
Country and type of partnership (if necessary)	Requirement to keep accounting records for partnerships formed under domestic law	Type of accounting records kept for partnerships formed under domestic law	Retention period for accounting records	Notes
Switzerland	Yes	Commercial Law: "Accounts required by the nature of its business in order to clearly state its financial situation." Tax Law: "An account of the takings, a statement of assets and debts, as well as an account of the expenditures and a statement of their personal investments."	10 years	
Turkey	Yes, a simple accounting method applies to certain merchants.	As required by the Accounting System General Communiqué and Tax Procedure Law.	10 years	
Turks and Caicos Islands	No, unless engaged in an activity requiring a license.	No, unless engaged in an activity requiring a license.	No, but if engaged in an activity requiring a license, 10 years.	
United Arab Emirates *Federal*	Yes	General partnerships and simple limited partnerships are required to keep a balance sheet and a profit/loss account.	As long as the partnership is valid.	Partnerships limited by shares have the same requirements as joint stock companies.
United Arab Emirates *DIFC General Partnerships*	Yes	The partnership is required to keep accounting records that are sufficient to show and explain its transactions. The partners are also required to keep accounts which show a true and fair view of the profit or loss for each financial year and the state of the financial affairs at the end of the financial year.	Until dissolution.	
United Arab Emirates *DIFC Limited Liability Partnerships DIFC Limited Partnerships*	Yes	The partnership is required to keep accounting records that are sufficient to show and explain its transactions and that may disclose with reasonable accuracy the financial position at any time and enable the members to ensure that any accounts prepared comply with legal requirements. The partnership is also required to keep accounts which show a true and fair view of the profit or loss for each financial year and the state of the financial affairs at the end of the financial year. The financial statements must be audited and filed.	10 years	

Table D.8   Accounting Information-Partnerships

1	2	3	4	5
Country and type of partnership (if necessary)	Requirement to keep accounting records for partnerships formed under domestic law	Type of accounting records kept for partnerships formed under domestic law	Retention period for accounting records	Notes
United Kingdom	Yes	Same as for other taxpayers.	5 years where a person carries on a trade, profession or business; otherwise 21 months except in the case of an enquiry.	
United States	Yes	To meet requirements of partnership and sufficient to explain the amount of gross income, deductions, credits or other amounts required to be shown in any return.	Yes, so long as the contents thereof may become material in the administration of any internal revenue law. Ordinarily this period would be a minimum of three years and frequently is indefinitely longer.	
United States Virgin Islands	Yes	To meet requirements of partnership and sufficient to explain the amount of gross income, deductions, credits or other amounts required to be shown in any return.	Yes, so long as the contents thereof may become material in the administration of any internal revenue law. Ordinarily this period would be a minimum of three years and frequently is indefinitely longer.	
Uruguay	Yes	Ledger, inventory book and copies of all documents.	20 years	
Vanuatu	Yes	Not specified.	No	

Table D.9
Accounting Information-Foundations

Explanation of column 2 through 4

This table dealing with foundations sets out whether there is a requirement to keep accounting records (**column 2**), the type of accounting records required to be kept (**column 3**) and the period of time such records must be retained (**column 4**).

Table D.9 Accounting Information-Foundations

1	2	3	4	5
Country and type of foundation (if necessary)	Requirement to keep accounting records for foundations formed under domestic law	Type of accounting records kept for foundations formed under domestic law	Retention period for accounting records	Notes
Argentina	Yes	Inventories, balance sheet, profit and loss account.	10 years	
Aruba	Yes	The books and records of a foundation must provide a proper insight into the assets and liabilities, rights and obligations of the foundation at all times.	10 years	
Austria	Yes	All records necessary for the determination of the tax liability.	7 years	
The Bahamas	Yes	Records regarding all sums of money received, expended and distributed, all sales and purchases and assets and liabilities of a foundation.	Minimum of 5 years is required for transaction records for anti-money laundering.	
Belgium	Yes	Same as for companies.	10 years	
Costa Rica	Yes	Statutory books, invoices and other documents supporting transactions.	4 years	
Czech Republic	Yes	Audited financial statements.	5 or 10 years	
Denmark	Yes	In such a way that all revenues and expenses are clear.	5 years	
Finland	Yes	All business transactions must be presented in order of recording and in systematic order. It must be possible at all times to control the completeness of the accounting entry posting and form an overall picture of the events, balance and result of the business activity. For every business transaction there must be a voucher. The foundation must draw up an annual report that gives a true and fair view of the enterprise's assets, liabilities and equity, financial position and results for the year. The annual report must be audited.	10 years	
France	Yes, if a foundation engages in an economic activity.	Balance sheet, profit and loss account and an annex on a yearly basis.	10 years	
Germany	Yes	Accounting records necessary to permit the calculation of taxable income.	10 years	If the foundation is engaged in a trade or business the accounting rules of the Commercial Code become applicable. Furthermore state laws may impose particular accounting requirements.

Table D.9   Accounting Information-Foundations

1	2	3	4	5
Country and type of foundation (if necessary)	Requirement to keep accounting records for foundations formed under domestic law	Type of accounting records kept for foundations formed under domestic law	Retention period for accounting records	Notes
Greece	Yes	In accordance with Code of Books and Data.	6 years	
Guatemala	Yes where a foundation carries on a business it must keep accounting records for tax purposes	Full accounting records.	4 years	
Hungary	Yes. Same as for companies.	Same requirements as for companies.	8/10 years	
Italy	Yes if carrying on business.	Same as those for other taxpayers carrying on business	10 years	
Japan	Yes	Inventory and other records.	10 years	
Korea	Yes for a welfare foundation.	Balance sheets, profit and loss statement and a certificate by a CPA.	No	
Liechtenstein	Yes	The rules that apply to companies also apply to foundations that carry out trade or business. Foundations that do not carry on trade or business have to maintain separate, correct, regular, clear and appropriate accounts, including where necessary supporting records.	10 years for foundations that carry out trade or business. Other foundations have to keep records on assets and liabilities but no specific retention period.	A licensed service provider on the foundation council of a foundation not engaged in commercial activities must make a statement to that effect and confirm that a statement of assets and liabilities is available.
Luxembourg	No	No	No	A foundation may be established solely for a public purpose.
Macao, China	Yes	Same obligation as public companies.	10 years	Same as for public companies.
Malta	Yes, if carrying on trade or business.	General tax rules apply.	9 years	Foundations, though recognised in case law and referred to in some laws, are not yet specifically regulated by legislation. Existing foundations are registered for income tax purposes.
Mexico	Yes	Sufficient to explain the amount of gross income, deductions, credits or other amounts required to be shown in any return.	5 years	
Monaco	Yes	Filing with the Minister of State of a report on a foundation's financial situation.	30 years	

Table D.9   Accounting Information-Foundations

1	2	3	4	5
Country and type of foundation (if necessary)	Requirement to keep accounting records for foundations formed under domestic law	Type of accounting records kept for foundations formed under domestic law	Retention period for accounting records	Notes
Netherlands	Yes, if it has business activities and satisfies a turnover criterion.	Same obligations as for companies.	7 years	
Netherlands Antilles	Yes	Records regarding everything that concerns business in accordance with the requirements of that business, in such a manner that from those records, the rights and obligations can at any time be ascertained.	10 years	
Norway	Yes	Financial statements.	3, 5 or 10 years depending on type of document.	
Panama	Yes	Sufficient to inform the beneficiaries of the state of its assets, as laid down in its charter or rules. If subject to tax in Panama they are required to file an income tax declaration and keep accounting records.	5 years	
Poland	Yes	Same standards as companies.	Permanently for approved financial statements; 5 years for other files.	
Portugal	Yes	A simplified accounting system.	10 years	Foundations must be constituted without a lucrative goal to pursue a general interest aim.
Russian Federation	No information.	No information.	No information.	
Saint Kitts and Nevis (applicable only in Nevis)	Yes	Books of account showing all sums of money received, expended and distributed by the Foundation and the matters in respect of which the receipt, expenditure and distribution take place; all sales and purchases; and the assets and liabilities of the Foundation.	6 years from the date on which they were made.	
San Marino	Yes	Same obligations as companies.	5 years	
Slovak Republic	Yes	Same obligations as companies.	5 years (10 years for financial statements and annual reports).	
Spain	Yes	Same requirements as companies.	6 years if carrying on business.	Foundations must be constituted without a lucrative goal to pursue a general interest aim.

Table D.9   Accounting Information-Foundations

1	2	3	4	5
Country and type of foundation (if necessary)	**Requirement to keep accounting records for foundations formed under domestic law**	**Type of accounting records kept for foundations formed under domestic law**	**Retention period for accounting records**	**Notes**
Sweden	Yes	All business transactions must be presented in order of recording and in systematic order. It must be possible at all times to control the completeness of the accounting entry posting and form an overall picture of the events, balance and result of the business activity. For every business transaction there must be a voucher. The foundation must draw up an annual report that gives a true and fair view of the enterprise's assets, liabilities and equity, financial position and results for the year. The annual report must be audited.	10 years	
Switzerland	Yes	For foundations engaged in a commercial activity, requirements are the same as for companies.	10 years for foundations engaged in commercial activities.	
Turkey	Yes	As required by the Accounting System General Communiqué and Tax Procedure Law.	5 years	If a foundation has an economic enterprise, relevant tax regulation applies to the enterprise.
Uruguay	Yes	Records must be kept on a uniform basis identifying each operation and justifying all expenses. An annual report of the foundation's financial situation must be made to the Government Ministry.	Indefinite	

OECD PUBLICATIONS, 2, rue André-Pascal, 75775 PARIS CEDEX 16
PRINTED IN FRANCE
(23 2007 11 1 P) ISBN 978-92-64-03902-5 – No. 55889 2007